ATLAS of the WORLD
with
GEOPHYSICAL BOUNDARIES

Figure 1: Atlas.

ATLAS

of the

WORLD

with

GEOPHYSICAL BOUNDARIES

showing

OCEANS, CONTINENTS and TECTONIC PLATES in their ENTIRETY

ATHELSTAN SPILHAUS

AMERICAN PHILOSOPHICAL SOCIETY

Independence Square · Philadelphia

1991

MEMOIRS OF THE
AMERICAN PHILOSOPHICAL SOCIETY
Held at Philadelphia
For Promoting Useful Knowledge

Volume 196

Library of Congress Catalog Card Number 91-55024
International Standard Book Number 0-87169-196-5
US ISSN 0065-9738

Acknowledgments

A number of people have generously given me help in the preparation of this atlas. I wish to acknowledge them and give them thanks.

John Snyder of the United States Geological Survey made my ideas digestible by a computer and continues his friendly collaboration.

Roger Goldsmith of Woods Hole Oceanographic Institution computerized and drew many of the maps in this atlas, often on very short notice.

Chuck Denham of Mathworks arranged the land movement data for Roger Goldsmith to use.

Woods Hole Oceanographic Institution gave me the opportunity to spend a summer working with its people. Special thanks go to Craig Dorman for inviting me; Jim Broadus, Arthur Gaines and Ethel LeFave for smoothing the way and Dave Ross and Judy Fenwick for their support and assistance.

Christopher Scotese of the University of Texas supplied data of his work in press on the movement of the landmasses through time.

The American Philosophical Society and in particular Herman Goldstine and Carole Le Faivre provided friendly critical appreciation of my work and made the publication of this atlas possible.

Above all, my wife, Kathy, assisted in everything from the most tedious chores to word processing, editing and understanding my involved material.

Table of Contents

List of Text Figures

World Maps of Oceans and Continents

SHORELINE MAPS:

TECTONIC PLATE MARGIN:

Atlas

The use of the name atlas for a collection of maps in a volume derives from a custom—initiated by Gerardus Mercator in the sixteenth century—of using as a frontispiece for such books the figure of the Titan, Atlas, holding the globe on his shoulders (FIG. 1).

It is a particularly appropriate title for this album of maps because the central feature of these maps is to show the world ocean, insofar as possible, uninterrupted by the edge of the map. Homer, in *The Odyssey*, states that Atlas is "one who knows the depths of the whole sea."[1]

Evolution of Projections

Mercator's original map was for seamen. Its marvelous property is that loxodromes, rhumb lines in navigation, are straight lines. Thus, a seaman can proceed along a plotted rhumb line by maintaining a constant bearing. The procedure of plotting the rhumb line is facilitated by the additional property of the Mercator map, that the latitude and longitude lines form a rectilinear graticule (grid) so that the appropriate bearing can be measured by an ordinary protractor.

In the intervening period, many excellent projections were developed and used to show the continents to best advantage in world maps. While they include the polar regions, because these were formerly untraveled and unknown, these regions were used as the points of maximum distortion. Mercator's map can never include the poles and retain its property of straight rhumb lines. Further, because interest centered on the continents, most world maps bisect the Pacific Ocean at the edges of the map.

Whole Ocean Maps

The author's original whole ocean map[2] was the first one after Mercator specifically designed for those interested in the sea and showed the world ocean uncut by the boundary of the map.

This first map of the whole ocean (MAP IA) achieved its purpose by selecting two antipodal points on earth on land and a half-great-circle joining these points, which passed almost entirely through land. This formed the edge of the map and the ocean was only cut at the Bering Strait.

---

[1] Homer, *The Odyssey*, line 52.

[2] Spilhaus, Athelstan, *Geographical Review*, 32:431–35, July, 1942.

Antipodal Shoreline Coincidences

It was possible to do this by the geographical coincidence of antipodal land. Antipodes are the parts of the globe diametrically opposite each other. Only about three percent of the surface of the earth is antipodal land (FIG. 2). The largest antipodal land occurs where the southern tip of South America is diametrically opposite eastern central Asia, including China. The old saw, that if children dug down through the center of the earth, they would come out in China would only be true if they started in the southern part of South America (FIG. 3).

The map of the antipodes (FIG. 2) shows us that the only continental shoreline coincidences near the Equator occur where South America is opposite Sumatra and Indonesia. Coincidences near the Equator are important because they give a more understandable, less oblique, aspect to the map. This is what makes this half-great-circle cut through land unique (FIG. 4).

In the first map of the whole ocean (MAP IA), while the ocean was complete, conventional practice was followed and the ellipse defined by the longitude and latitude graticule was used as the edge of the map. As a result, the continents of the Americas and Eurasia are intersected by the edge of the map. Where previous cartographers cut the oceans to see the land, now the land was cut to see the oceans.

It then became apparent that nothing demanded that the edge of a map need be a smooth curve dictated by the tremendously useful yet artificial graticule of latitude and longitude.

Extended Graticules

Freed from the confines of latitude and longitude lines, the edges of the maps could be the natural, physical boundaries of ocean and land—the shorelines. To accommodate the shorelines, the conventional one-world graticule is allowed to overrun (FIGS. 5 and 6). The extended graticule permits the shorelines of the continents to be delineated so that the edge of the map is a natural boundary[3] (MAP I).

> He had bought a large map representing the sea,
> > Without the least vestige of land:
> And the crew were much pleased when they found it to be
> > A map they could all understand.
>
> "What's the good of . . .
> > . . . zones and meridian lines?"
> So the bellman would cry; and the crew would reply,
> > "They are merely conventional signs!"[4]
>
> Geographers emphasize from where they stand
> > That the land is encircled by sea.
> But the crew now perceives, what to them is just grand,
> > That land is mere periphery!"[5]

---

[3] Spilhaus, Athelstan, and Snyder, John P., "World Maps with Natural Boundaries," *Cartography and Geographic Information Systems*, in press.

[4] Carroll, Lewis, "The Hunting of the Snark," Fit the Second, Stanzas 2 and 3.

[5] Spilhaus, (long) after Lewis Carroll.

Figure 2: Map of the world showing antipodal continental land and continental shoreline antipodal coincidences.

Figure 3: Antipodes are points on earth opposite each other.
Needle through China pierces South America.

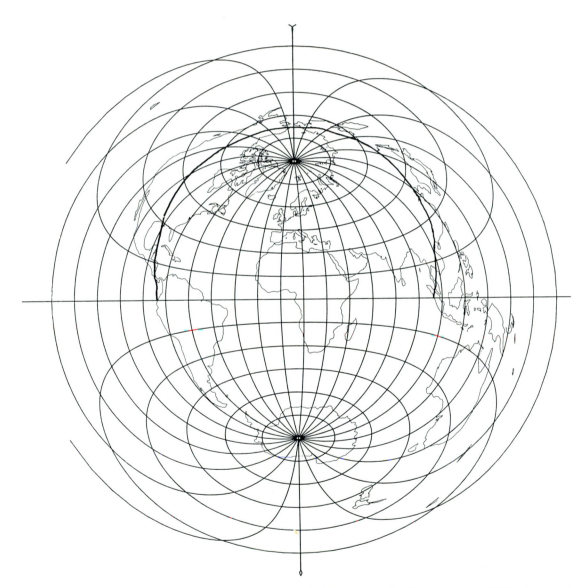

Figure 4: Continental shorelines from the west coast of South America on the Equator through North America and the east coast of Asia to Sumatra on the Equator are cut by the ocean only at the Bering and Malacca Straits. The shorelines closely follow a half-great-circle.

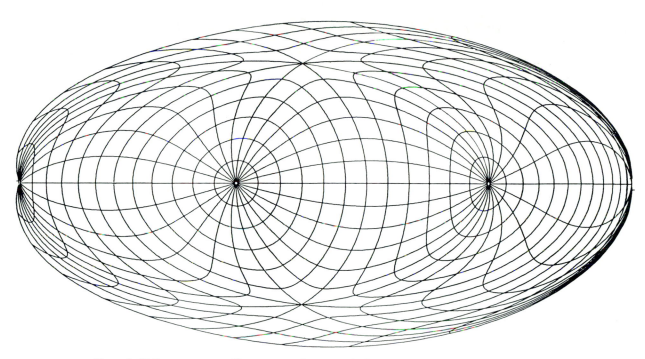

Figure 5: Oblique transverse Hammer equal area graticule extended to encompass "1 ½" worlds.

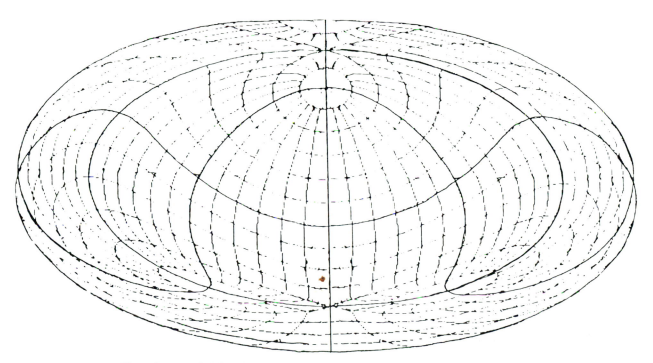

Figure 6: Normal oblique Hammer equal area graticule extended beyond one world.

Narrowest Junctions of the Three Oceans

So far, the two guiding principles for maps with physical boundaries have been shore-line boundaries requiring the use of antipodal shoreline coincidences and overrunning the conventional one-world graticule to avoid cutting the continents. There is a third guide-line that should be applied. When it is necessary for the edge of the map to cut the sea, the cut should be at the narrowest junctions between two of the three lobes of the world ocean.

For equatorial aspects of world maps with physical boundaries, one must choose, as the location for one of the cuts, the Drake Passage between Cape Horn and the tip of the Palmer Peninsula[6] in Antarctica; the ocean between Cape Agulhas, the southernmost tip of Africa, down the 20° E. meridian to the coast of Antarctica, or the sea between Sumatra on the equator through the Sunda Strait and east along the chain of islands to the easternmost point of Timor thence to Darwin, Australia, and across the Bass Strait through Tasmania along the 147° E. meridian to the coast of Antarctica (FIG. 7).

The narrowest of the three ocean connections in the Southern Hemisphere dividing the world ocean into its three lobes—the Pacific, the Atlantic and the Indian Oceans—is the Drake Passage. The equatorial aspect of the world map (MAP IV) on the extended graticule shows the ocean cut only at the Drake Passage. The poles of the map are the shoreline antipodal coincidences in Alaska and Antarctica.

The Parent Projections

For the majority of maps in this atlas, the Hammer Projection has been used as the parent projection when the property preserved is equal area or equivalence. For continental shoreline boundaries, as there is no continental shoreline coincidence at the North and South geographical poles, the normal projection cannot be used.

Various aspects of the Hammer Projection (FIG. 8), by moving the poles of the map at 45° intervals and the center by 45° intervals, clarify the terms normal, oblique normal, transverse normal, oblique transverse, centered transverse, centered oblique and oblique. In accepted cartographical nomenclature, only three terms—normal, transverse and oblique—are generally employed. This sometimes leads to confusion, especially with reference to oblique projections.[7]

Oblique normal projections are centered on the straight central prime meridian of the normal projection at any latitude other than 90° or 0° and have projection poles on that meridian 90° of latitude from the center.

Oblique transverse projections are centered on the straight Equator of the normal projection at any longitude other than 90° or 0° and have projection poles on the 90th meridian.

---

[6] It is reckless to use geographical names because they are subject to change by the gusts of political wind. For example, the Palmer Peninsula is now sometimes known as the Antarctic Peninsula.

[7] Snyder, John P., and Voxland, Philip M., *An Album of Map Projections*, U.S. Geological Survey, Professional Paper 1453, U.S. Gov. Printing Office, 1989. In the Glossary, oblique aspect is defined as the "aspect of a projection on which the center of projection or origin is located at a point which is neither at a pole nor along the equator." However, the map on page 42 of the *Album* shows an "oblique sinusoidal projection," although the center of the projection is, indeed, on the equator. With the nomenclature here, this would be a centered oblique sinusoidal projection.

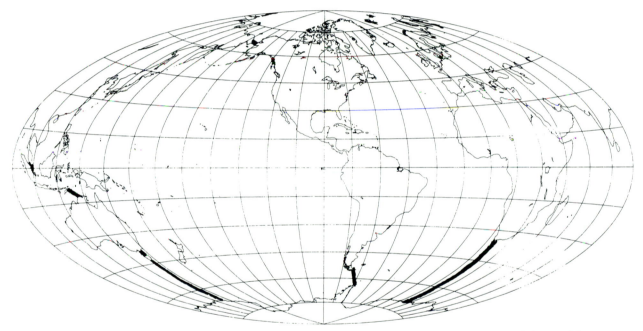

Figure 7: Map of the world showing the shortest ocean connections linking the three parts of the world ocean.

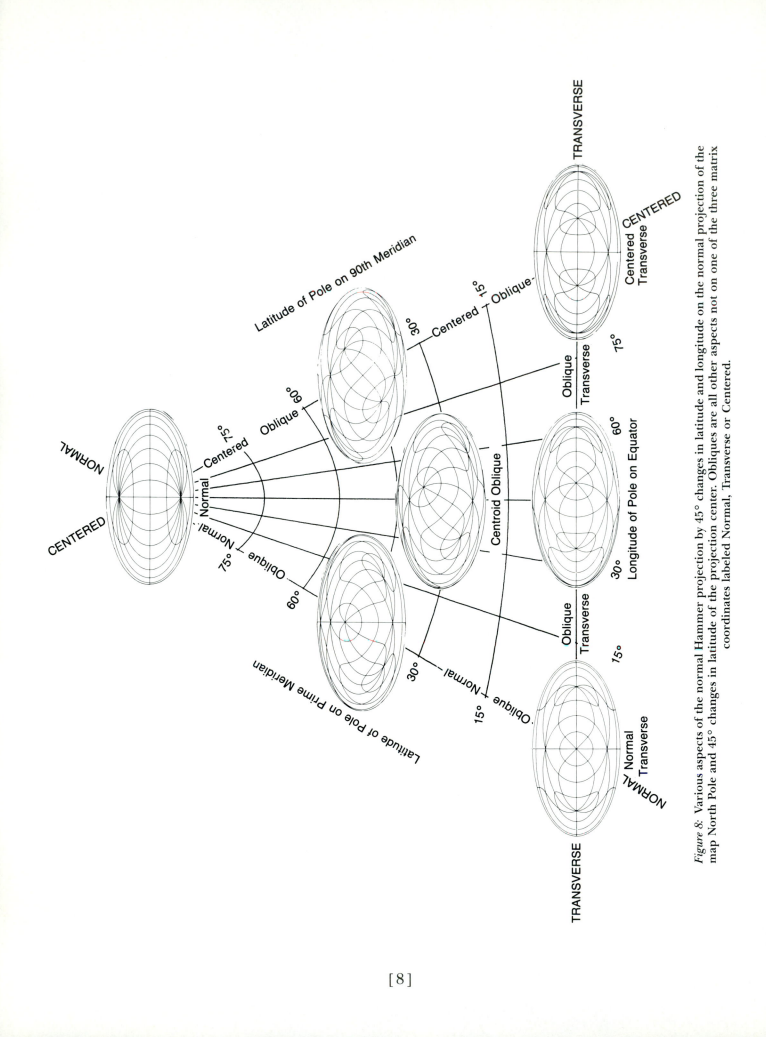

Figure 8: Various aspects of the normal Hammer projection by 45° changes in latitude and longitude on the normal projection of the map North Pole and 45° changes in latitude of the projection center. Obliques are all other aspects not on one of the three matrix coordinates labeled Normal, Transverse or Centered.

Centered oblique projections are centered at 0° latitude on the central prime meridian at the Equator and have projection poles on the 90th meridian of the normal projection.

Oblique projections have centers and projection poles neither on the Equator nor on either the prime central meridian or on the 90th meridian (FIG. 9).

This nomenclature developed as necessity arose in the preparation of this atlas. It employs only one new qualifying term, "centered," and combinations of the well known terms for the other nonorthogonal aspects. The nomenclature suggested by Thomas Wray[8] could have been used for the four nonorthogonal aspects but it introduces four new terms, i.e., first transverse, second transverse, equiskew and skew.

Many projections (MAPS I–VII, XII, XXII–XXV and XXVII–XXIX) in this atlas have the property of being equal area and the Hammer is used as the parent projection in its various aspects, other than the normal (FIG. 8).

Although the Hammer Projection was selected here, other equal area projections (Sinusoidal, Mollweide, Boggs, Craster, Quartic, Adams and Eckert-Greifindorff) could be chosen as the parent projection, if desired. Some compromise projections (neither equal area nor conformal) could also be used. These are Aitoff, (MAP XX); Putnins P₅ and von de Grinten IV.

For some purposes, it is desirable to use conformal map projections. Conformal map projections, instead of preserving the property of equivalent areas, have the lines of latitude and longitude on the map graticule intersect at right angles and preserve shape at each point on earth. (It may be mentioned that though the Mercator is not a world map it does have the property of conformality.)

Conformal maps of whatever projection are characterized by increasing distortion of size as you move from the center of the map. However, because the meridians and parallels of the graticule intersect at right angles, the conformal map may be preferred for showing vector quantities where direction, as of an ocean current or a wind, is to be portrayed (MAP VIII). This map has the identical center and poles of the equal area map (MAP II) but preserves conformality rather than equivalence of area.

Similarly, a conformal version of the equatorial aspect (MAP IX) with the same poles and center as Map IV is shown. This map may at first appear a shocking distortion when the size of South America and North America are regarded. However, when compared to the Mercator, it must be remembered that this is a map of the whole world, including the poles which would be infinitely distorted by the Mercator projection.

For the conformal versions, the August Epicycloidal Projection (MAP IXA) has been used but, again, other well known conformal projections of the world, such as Adams elliptical conformal, could serve as the parent projections for these maps.

There is an intrinsic beauty in uninterrupted pictures of the whole world and here we have added to that by not interrupting the continents or the world ocean by the edges of the map. However, as examination of these maps show, the areas on the edge of the maps are often elongated or distorted. In order to improve the shapes of continents and oceans, cartographers have used interrupted maps.

---

[8] Wray, Thomas, "The Seven Aspects of a General Map Projection," Monograph No. 11/1974, *Cartographica*, Supplement No. 2 to "Canadian Cartographer," Vol. 11, 1974, University of Toronto Press. John Snyder drew the author's attention to this work in a personal communication.

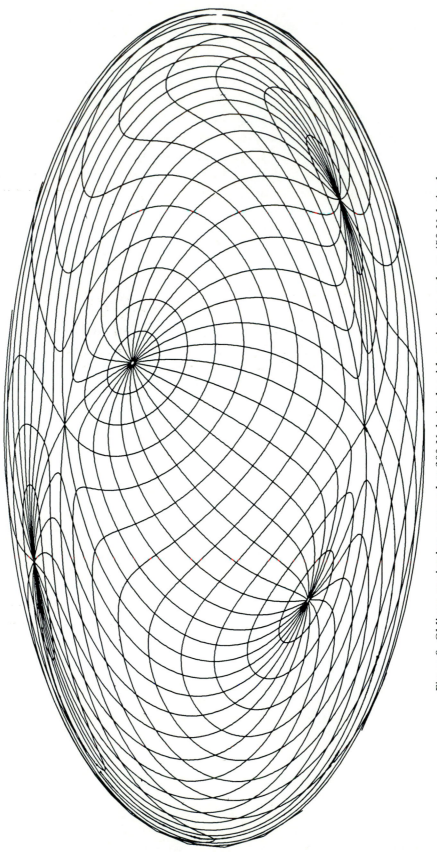

Figure 9: Oblique projection centered at 30° N. latitude with projection pole at 45° N. latitude.

The system of natural boundaries may also be used to generate interrupted world maps with natural boundaries. Interruptions improve the shape because there is less distortion in depicting, on a flat surface, a lune[9] or gore of a sphere than the entire surface of a sphere. However, such interruptions, in themselves, detract from the unity of the whole earth which we attempt to portray. The interruptions in this atlas at least have the merit of being along natural boundaries.

The Maps in This Atlas

The atlas of world maps is divided into three parts: maps with continental shorelines as natural boundaries; composite maps with continental shorelines as natural boundaries; maps with tectonic plate margins as natural boundaries.

All graticules on the illustrations are 15° spacing unless otherwise noted and can be computer drawn. All projections, including land masses and plates, are suitable for computer drawing although, in some cases, some data have been entered by hand.

Latitudes and longitudes are given for the poles of the map and for the center of the map. Latitudes are expressed in degrees north or south of the Equator; longitudes are given in degrees east or west of the Greenwich Meridian. This information is sufficient to specify the aspect of the projection.

Note that the poles of the map are the continental shoreline coincidences or plate boundary coincidences chosen for the particular map.

---

[9] Lune, n., the part of a spherical surface bounded by two great circles.

Maps with Continental Shorelines as Natural Boundaries

Maps I to XI

SHORELINE MAP I

Oblique transverse Hammer equal area with projection poles at Equator, 80° W. and Equator, 100° E.; center at 66.5° S., 10° E. (10° graticule).

This is an extended graticule version with straight central meridian of the original World Ocean Equal Area Map (MAP IA, Spilhaus, 1942), with continents in their entirety.

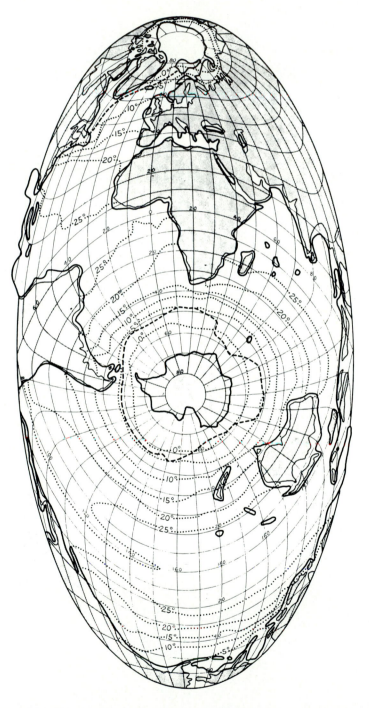

MAP IA: World ocean map Hammer equal area projection showing mean temperature of the sea surface. Heavy broken line shows extreme limit of sea ice, heavy full line, 200-meter isobath (10° graticule).

MAP I

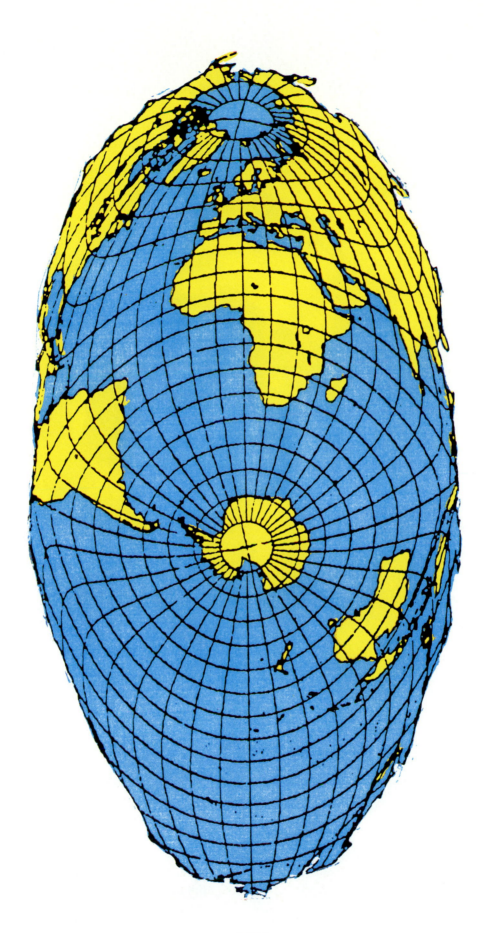

SHORELINE MAP II

Oblique Hammer equal area with projection poles at 7.5° S., 79.5° W. and 7.5° N., 100.5° E.; center at 66.5° S., 10.5° E.

This is a "purist" version of Map I. In Map I, the edge of the map cuts both the Bering Strait and the Malacca Strait. In this map, only the Bering Strait is cut.

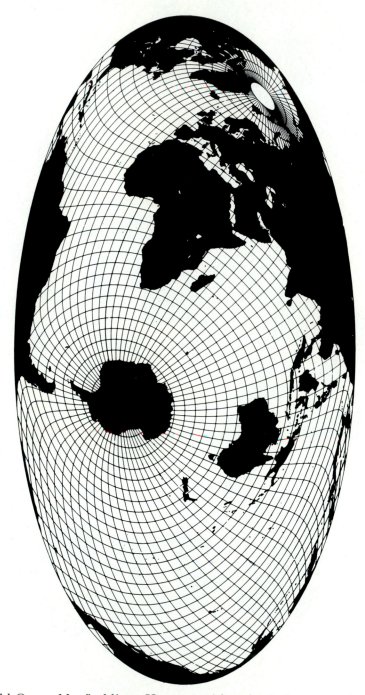

MAP IIA: "World Ocean Map," oblique Hammer with poles in largest antipodal land masses, South America and China, Spilhaus, 1974.

MAP II

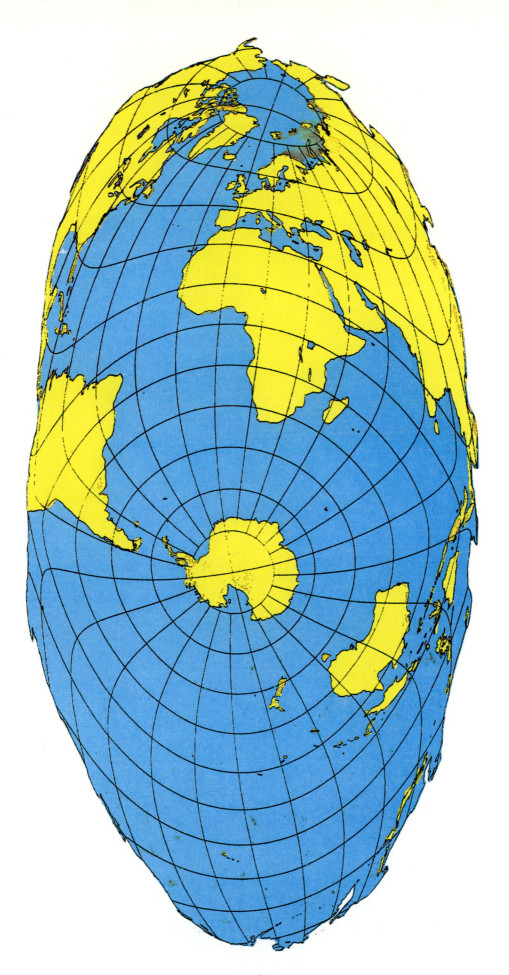

SHORELINE MAP III

Centered transverse Hammer equal area with projection poles at Equator, 80° W.; Equator, 100° E.; center at Equator, 10° E.

Bartholomew's "Atlantis" projection (MAP IIIA) is a land version of the World Ocean Map (MAP IA). It was designed to highlight the lands and the Atlantic Ocean but, to do so, the edge of the map cuts the other oceans severely.

In Map III, the continents are shown in their entirety, as are the oceans, with ocean cuts only at the Bering and Malacca Straits. This projection is also useful for the portrayal of tectonic plates (MAP XXV, XXVII–XXIX). The graticule, extended to include "1½" worlds, is portrayed unclipped around the edge of the continents.

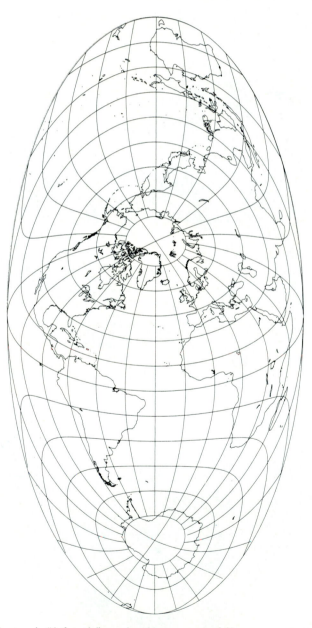

MAP IIIA: Bartholomew's "Atlantis" projection on an oblique transverse Mollweide, 1958.

MAP III

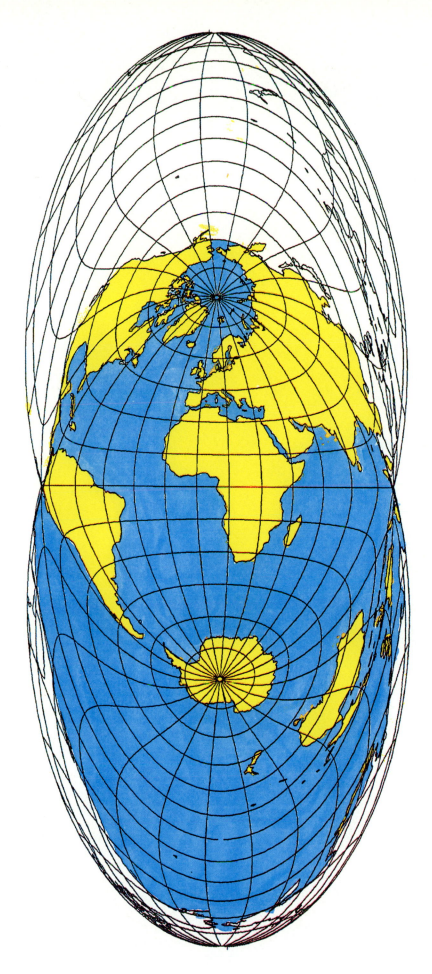

SHORELINE MAP IV

Centered oblique Hammer equal area with projection poles at 69.5° N., 163° W.; 69.5° S., 17° E.; center at Equator, 107° E.

This map is an equatorial view and the ocean is cut at the Drake Strait only. Whereas Maps I, II and III used shoreline coincidences on or near the Equator to achieve a polar aspect, the coincidences of the northern shores of North America and Asia with antipodal points on the shoreline of Antarctica are used in this map.

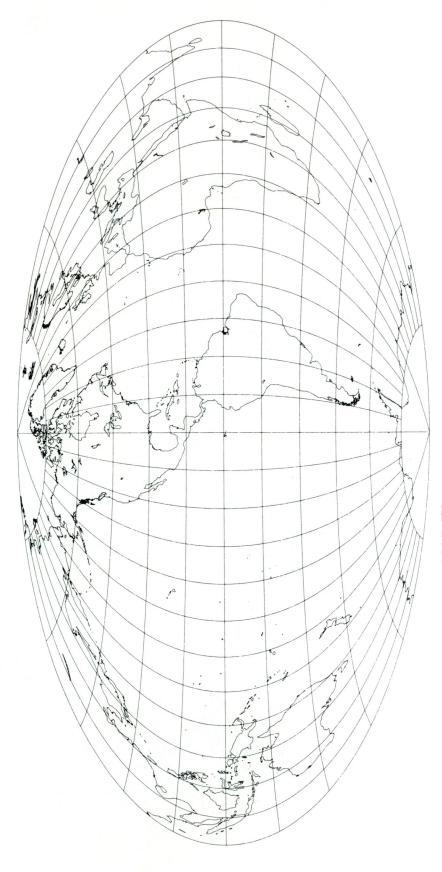

MAP IVA: Normal Hammer projection.

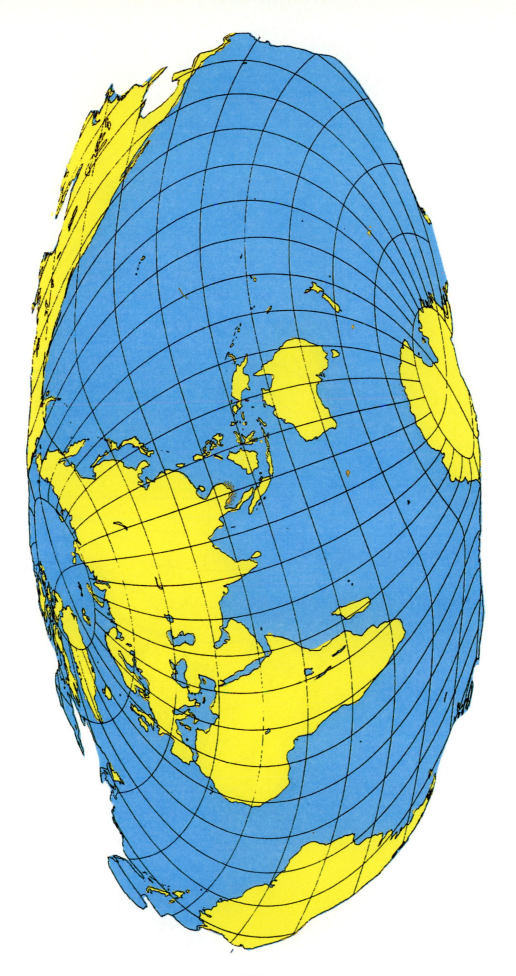

MAP IV

SHORELINE MAP V

Oblique normal Hammer equal area with projection poles at 77.75° N., 105° W.; 77.75° S., 75° E; center at 12.25° S., 105° E.

This equatorial view is shown to demonstrate the versatility of the system of using shoreline boundaries. It has a straight central meridian and shows Antarctica to good advantage.

In Map VA is an equatorial view of the world with the Pacific in the center of the map and with ocean cuts across the Bering Strait and from Africa to Antarctica.

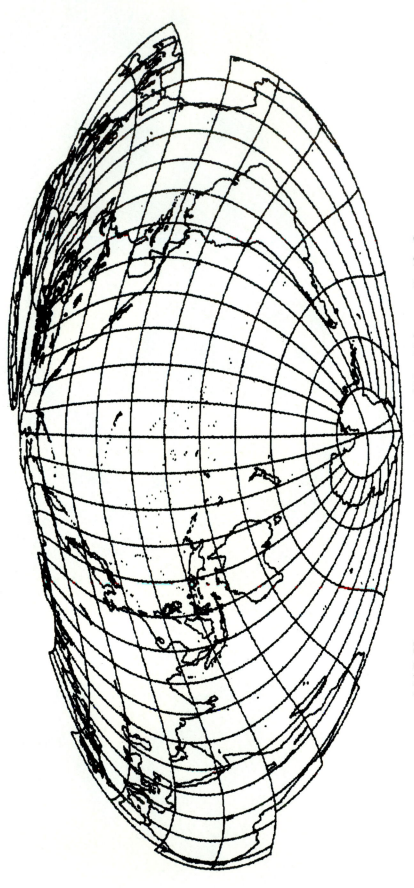

MAP VA: Unclipped alternative arrangement of Map V features Pacific Ocean.

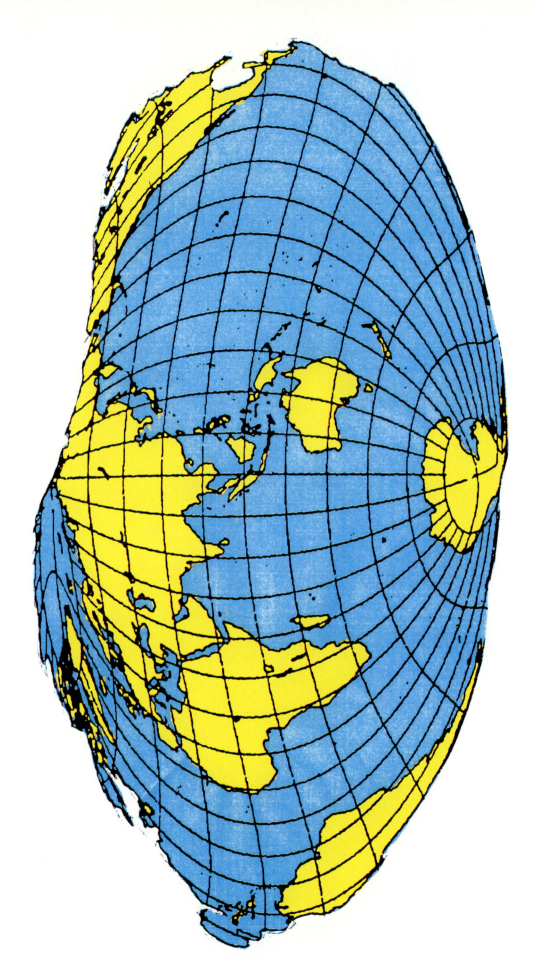

MAP V

SHORELINE MAP VI

Oblique normal Hammer equal area with projection poles at 67° N., 85° W.; 67° S., 95° E.; center at 13° N., 95° E. (10° graticule).

This is a different equatorial view with the ocean cut at the Drake Strait only. In comparison to Map V, this shows the Arctic to good advantage at the expense of distortion in the Antarctic.

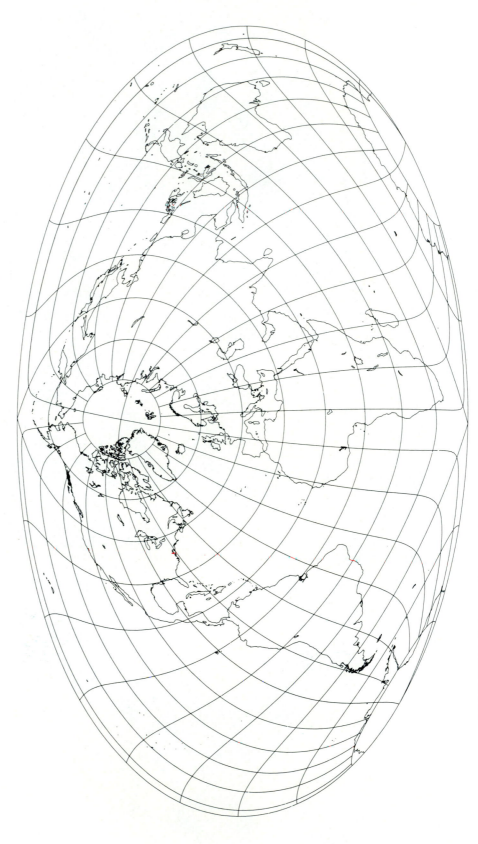

MAP VIA: Briesemeister projection, modified oblique normal Hammer, center at 45° N., 10° E.

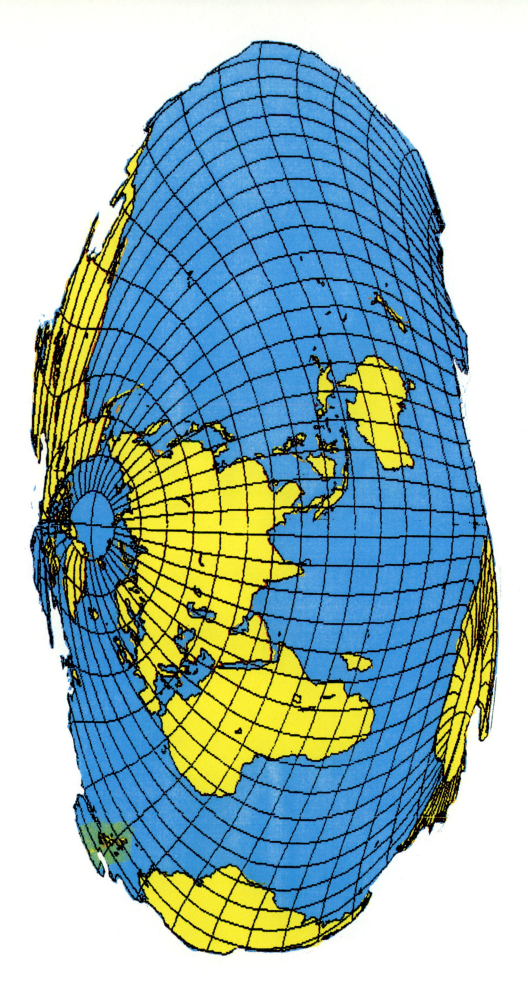

MAP VI

SHORELINE MAP VII

This projection is identical to Map IV with State Department data entered by computer. This use of the map demonstrates the territorial sea limits, 200 miles from any land. This 200 mile limit was one geographical basis in the discussions in the Law of the Sea Conference.

For comparison, the same limits are shown in Maps VIIA and VIIB. It will be readily seen that the Mercator projection does not show the 200-mile isopleth in the Arctic Ocean and severely distorts areas so that one cannot visually compare areas of territorial waters in one part of the world with another. The McBryde Projection corrects this latter fault but cuts the Arctic.

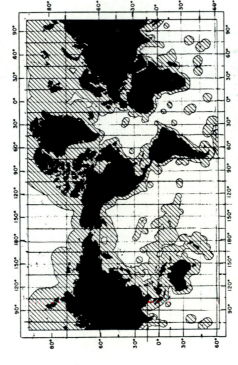

MAP VIIA: 200-mile isopleths on a Mercator projection, U.S. State Department.

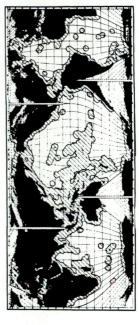

MAP VIIB: 200-mile isopleths on equal area sectional projection, McBryde.

[26]

MAP VII

SHORELINE MAP VIII

Oblique August conformal with projection poles at 7.5° S., 79.5° W.; 7.5° N., 100.5° E.; center at 66.5° S., 10.5° E.

Conformal version of Map II with ocean cut at the Bering Strait only. This is an extended graticule version of the original world ocean conformal map (MAP VIIIA, Spilhaus, 1942), with continents in their entirety.

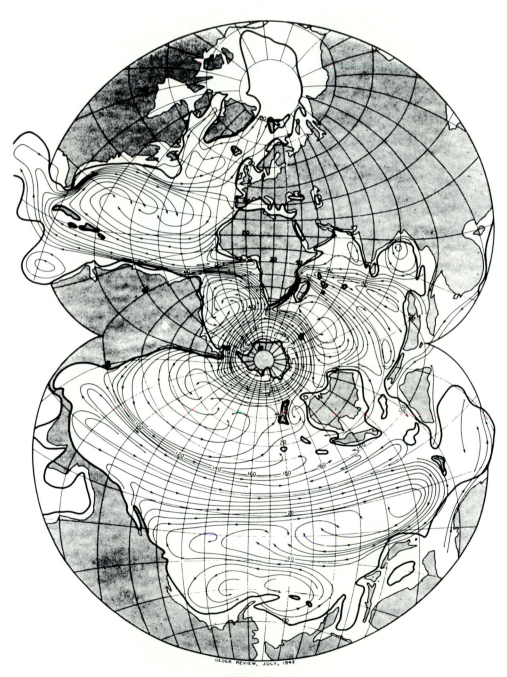

MAP VIIIA: "World Ocean Map," oblique transverse August conformal projection showing ocean currents in the northern hemisphere winter. Heavy full line, 200-meter isobath (10° graticule).

[28]

MAP VIII

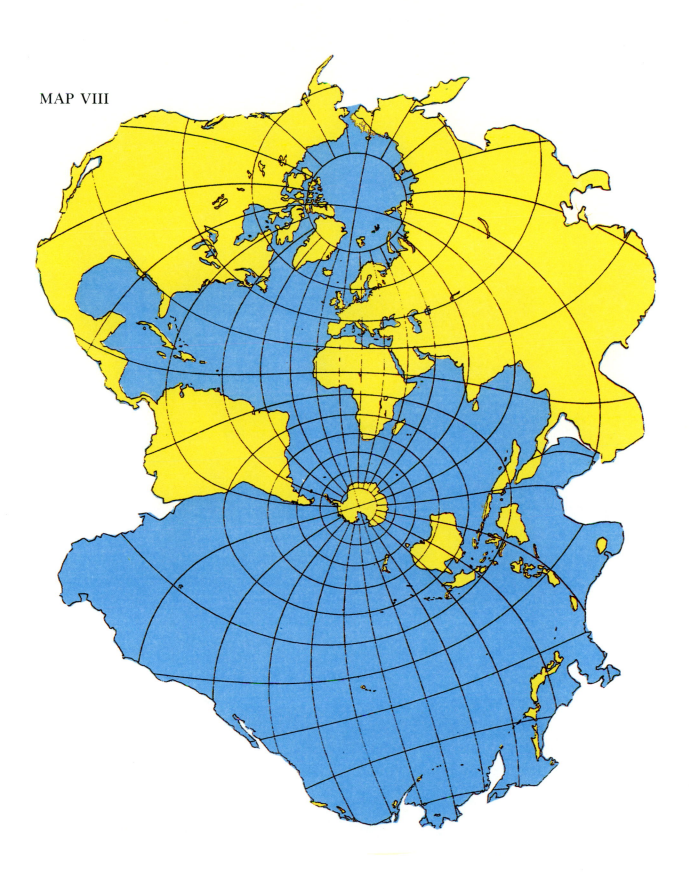

SHORELINE MAP IX

Centered oblique August conformal with projection poles at 69.5° N., 163° W.; 69.5° S., 17° E.; center at Equator, 107° E.

Conformal version with the same projection poles and center as Map IV with ocean cut at Drake Strait only.

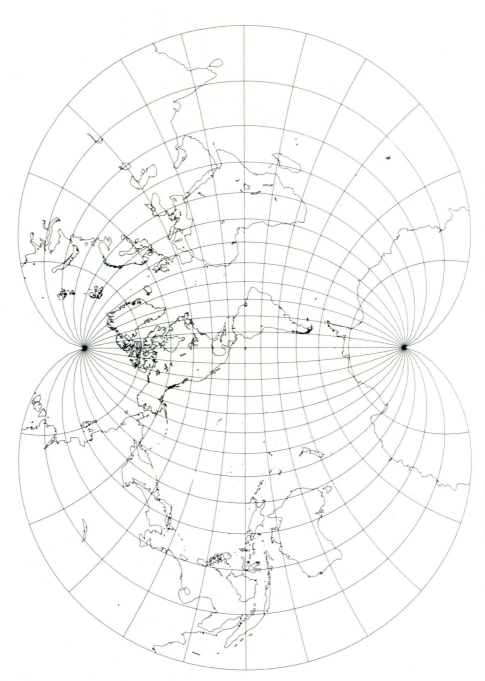

MAP IXA: Normal August epicycloidal conformal projection.

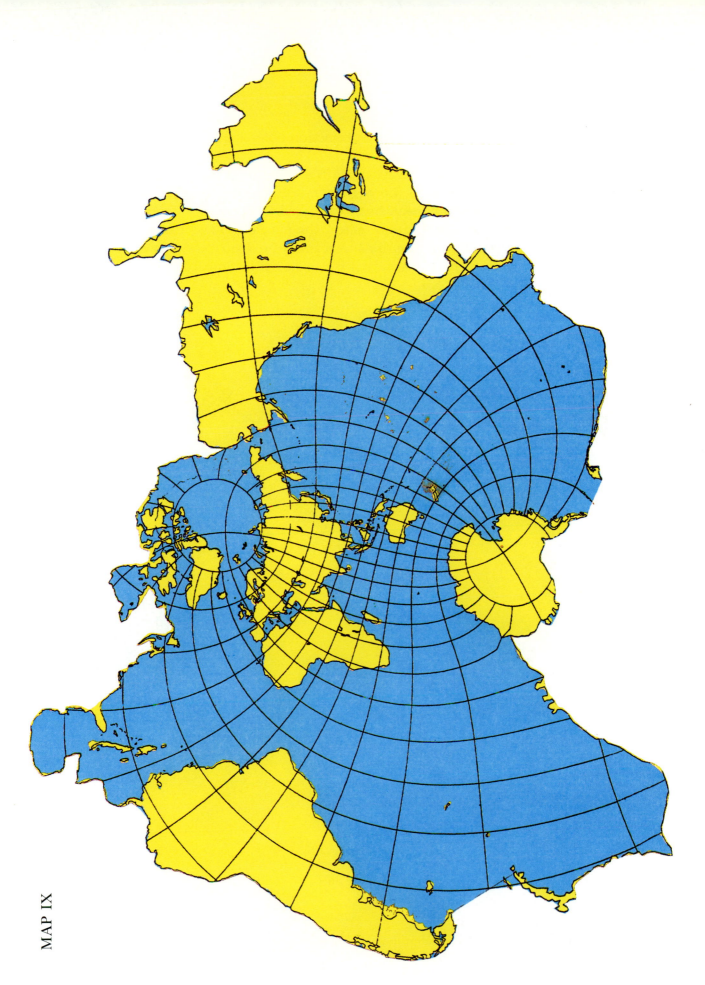

MAP IX

SHORELINE MAP X

Oblique normal August conformal with projection poles at 77.75° N., 105° E.; 77.75° S., 75° W.; center at 12.25° S., 105° E.

This conformal map cuts the ocean at the Bering and Drake Straits only. As in all conformal projections, the areas on the periphery are greatly enlarged. In this case, it is most noticeable in the Arctic Ocean but, compared to the Lagrange (MAP XA) where both Arctic and Antarctic are large and bisected, the map may have advantages. The displacement of North America from South America may be disturbing. However, it simply emphasizes that the bulk of North America is not north of South America.

MAP XA: Normal Lagrange conformal projection of a sphere in a circle with center at Equator, 90° W.

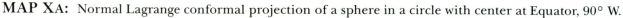

MAP X

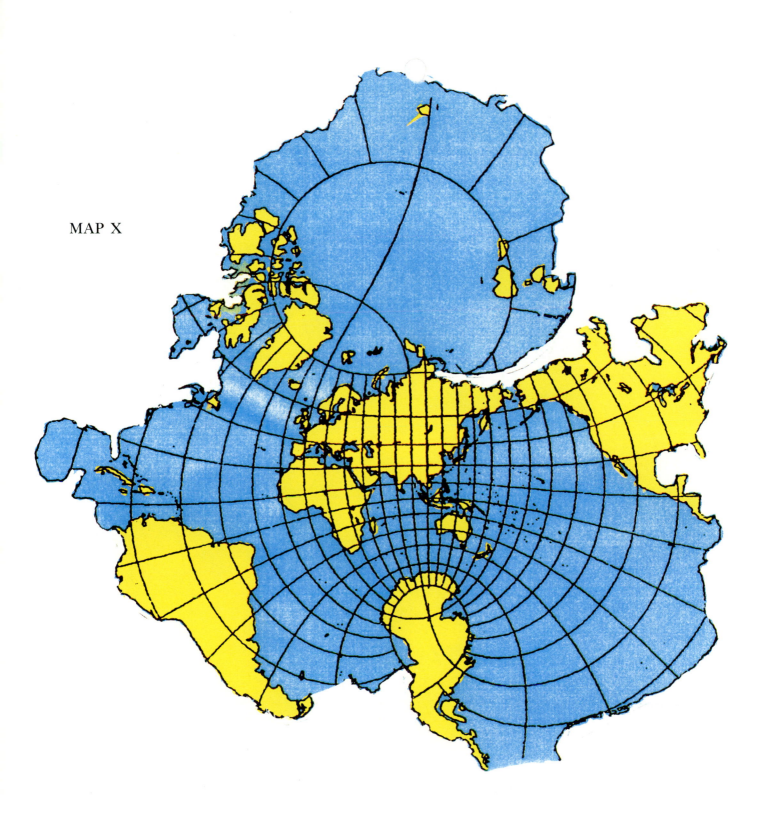

SHORELINE MAP XI

Oblique normal stereographic conformal with center at 45° S., 95° W.

This is not a world map as the stereographic projection goes to infinity at the antipode of its center. This antipode, 45° N., 85° E., is a point in the continent of Asia approximately farthest from any ocean. The ocean is uncut and in its entirety but only the shoreline of Asia, which forms the edge of the map, is shown. Omitting Asia is similar to omitting the polar regions on a Mercator map. The same map on a Lambert equal area projection, while not omitting Asia, confines it to a thin band encircling the map (MAP XIA).

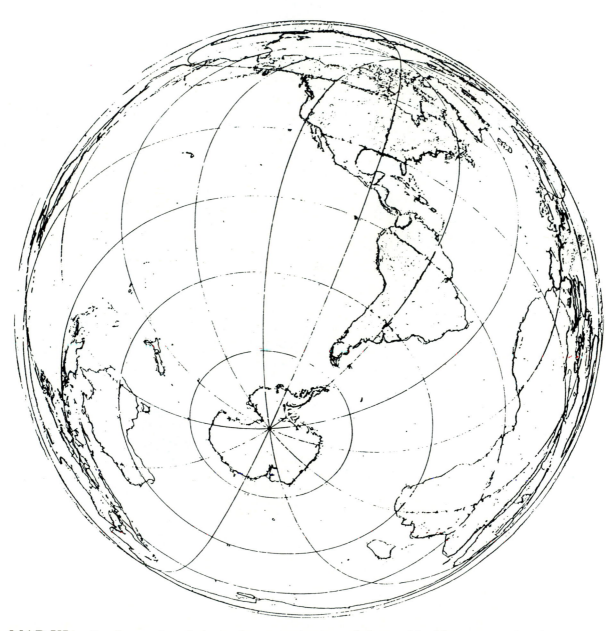

MAP XIA: Lambert azimuthal equal area projection of the world with center at 45° S., 95° W.

[34]

MAP XI

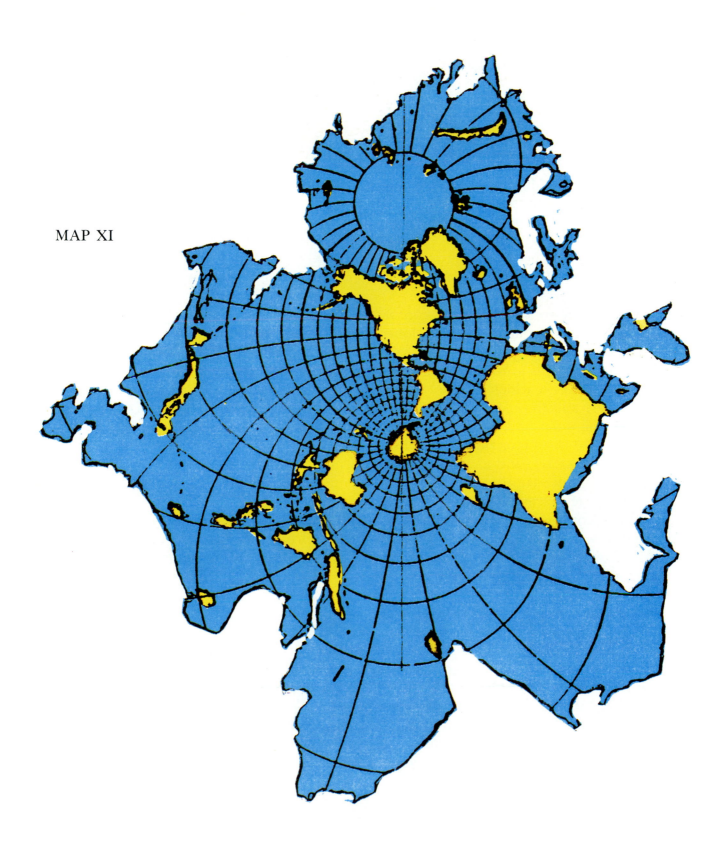

Interrupted World Maps with Natural Boundaries

The Shoreline Maps (MAPS I–XI) are framed around the perimeter by continental shorelines and short ocean passages. However, the continents near the periphery of these maps are often distorted. The justification for interrupted maps is to minimize the distortion of the shapes of continents and oceans. In interrupted versions, the world is divided into segments which are assembled into a whole. The Composite Shoreline Maps (MAPS XII–XXI) are examples of new forms of world maps interrupted along the shorelines—the natural boundaries.

As there are three principal oceans which join around Antarctica, the most obvious form is a three-lobed map with each lobe encompassing one of the three oceans and its adjacent continents. In 1983, a nearly equal area map of the world ocean along these lines was produced.[10] This world map comprised three segments but the segments were joined using artistic license which violated the strictly equal area property of the map (MAP XIIA).

It is desirable, however, that the map have mathematical exactitude so that it can be drawn by computer and so that entries to be made on the map can be entered by computer. This led to an interrupted world map of three lobes (irregular lunes) with natural boundaries (MAP XII) and a companion conformal version (MAP XIII).[11]

The deep interruptions to the South Pole in these three-lobed maps cut the world ocean in three places in the Southern Hemisphere.

In an effort to eliminate the three cuts in the southern ocean, a sinusoidal equal area projection was employed (MAP XIV). The sinusoidal projection has the unique property that both meridians and parallels are equally spaced along the Equator and along the central meridian. It is this feature that makes possible a class of segmented interrupted sinusoidal world maps (MAPS XIV–XIX).

There are various ways of joining segments of normal and transverse sinusoidal graticules to form interrupted world maps. This property permits segments of two transverse sinusoidal maps whose central meridians are 90° apart to be fitted together with perfect accuracy and preserving strictly the equal area property. Also, segments of normal and transverse sinusoidal projections with different central meridians may be combined.

The equal area sinusoidal is the parent projection employed in these maps. However, there are compromise projections that have equal spacing along both the central meridian and parallel. Aitoff (MAP XX); Putnin P_5 and v.d. Grinten IV may be used in a similar manner. Using the principles embodied here, many other variations of composite interrupted maps may be produced.

---

[10] Spilhaus, Athelstan, "World Ocean Maps: The Proper Places to Interrupt," *Proceedings of the American Philosophical Society*, Vol. 127, No. 1, 1983, p. 58.

[11] Spilhaus and Snyder, "World Maps with Natural Boundaries."

Composite Maps with Continental Shorelines
as Natural Boundaries

Maps XII to XXI

COMPOSITE SHORELINE MAP XII

Interrupted three-lobed oblique transverse Hammer equal area with lobe projections centered at latitude 66.5° S. and longitudes at 50° W. (Atlantic), 70° E. (Indian), 170° W. (Pacific). Projection poles are on Equator, 90° E. and 90° W. of each central meridian.

This is a true equal area version of the nearly equal area "Map of the World Ocean" (MAP XIIA, Spilhaus, 1983).

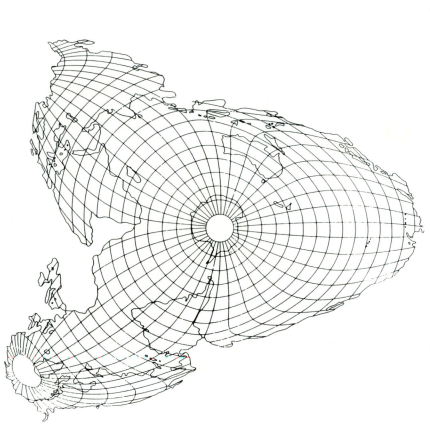

MAP XIIA: "World Ocean Map," (not computer drawn), approximately equal area.

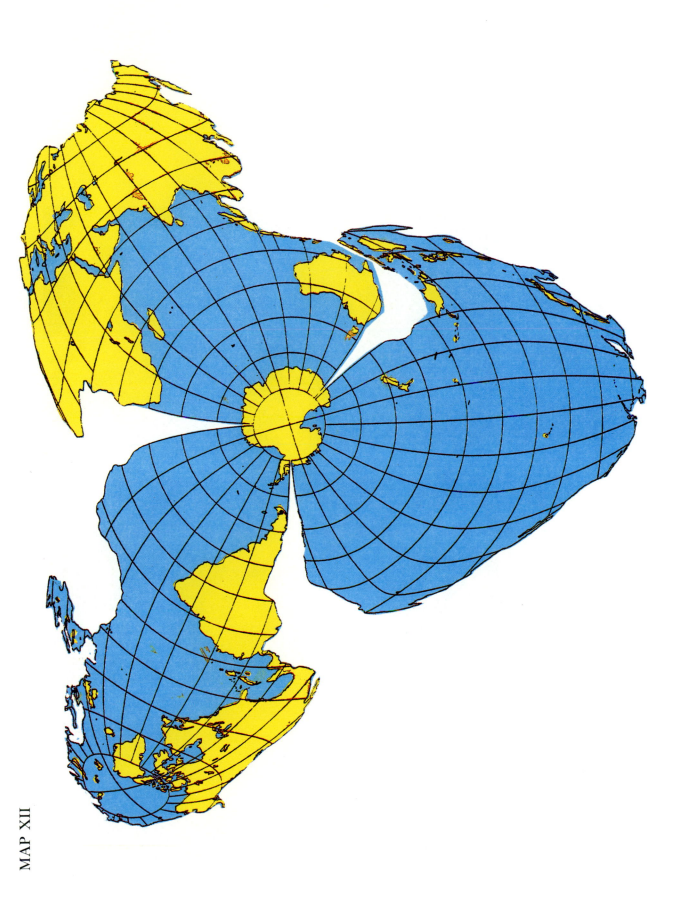

MAP XII

COMPOSITE SHORELINE MAP XIII

Interrupted three-lobed oblique transverse August conformal with lobe projections centered at latitude 66.5° S. and longitudes at 50° W. (Atlantic), 70° E. (Indian), 170° W. (Pacific). Projection poles are on Equator, 90° E. and 90° W. of each central meridian. This is a conformal version of Map XII.

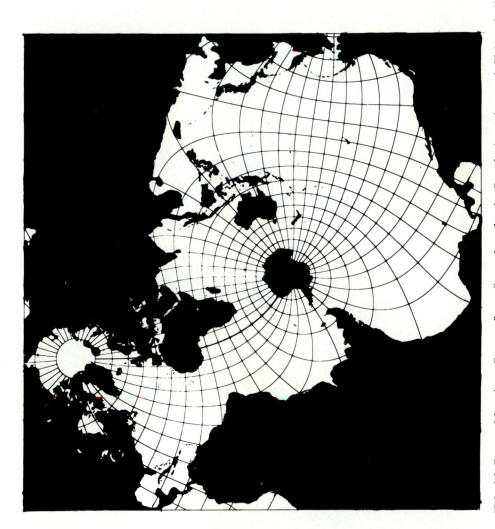

MAP XIIIA: "World Ocean Map in a Square," conformal, poles in South America and China, Spilhaus, 1979.

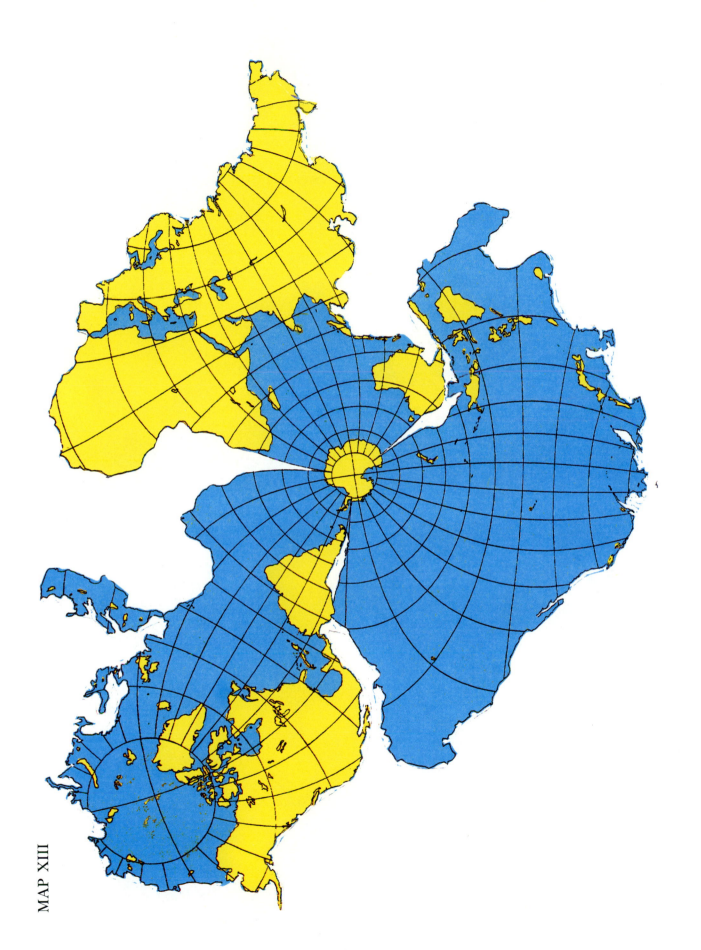

MAP XIII

COMPOSITE SHORELINE MAP XIV

Composite of two normal transverse sinusoidal equal area projections with lobes centered at 90° S. (South Pole) and central meridians 10° E.–170° W. and 80° W.–100° E. Projection poles are on the Equator 90° E. and 90° W. of central meridians (10° graticule). Cuts the ocean at the Bering and Malacca Straits.

This composite eliminates the three deep ocean cuts in Map XII. It is a computer drawn equal area version of Map XIVA.

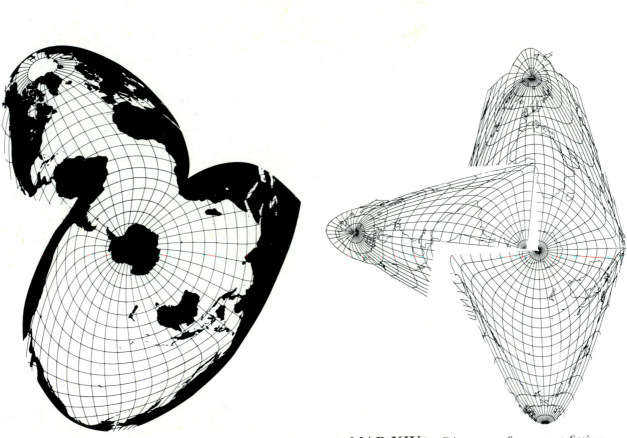

MAP XIVA: Approximate equal area composite (Spilhaus, 1979).

MAP XIVB: Diagram of segment fitting.

MAP XIV

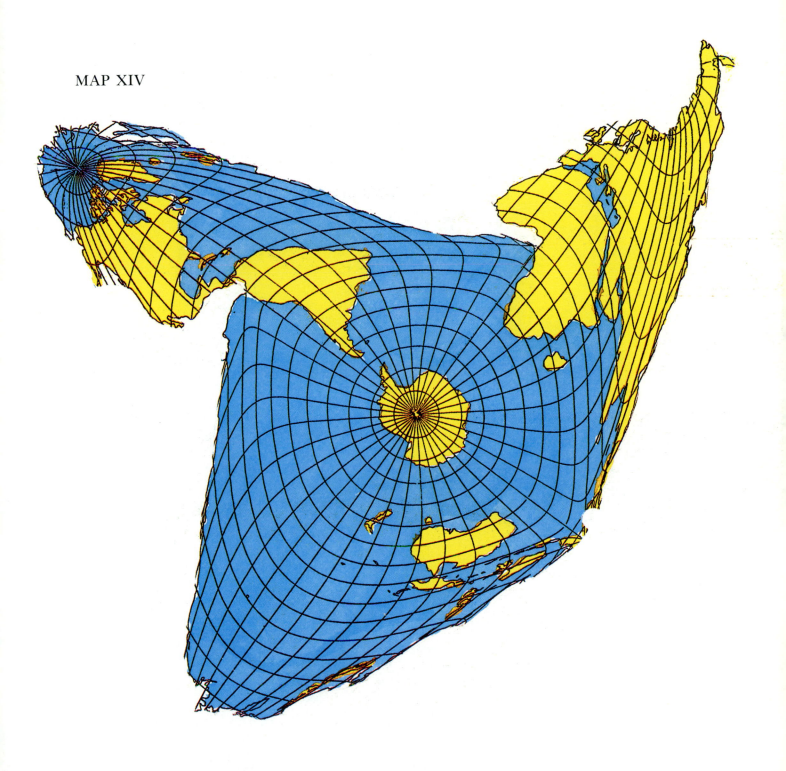

COMPOSITE SHORELINE MAP XV

Composite of two normal transverse sinusoidal equal area projections with lobes centered at 90° N. (North Pole) and central meridians 10° E.–170° W. and 80° W.–100° E. Projection poles are on the Equator, 90° E. and 90° W. of central meridians (10° graticule). Cuts the ocean from Africa to Antarctica, Malay Peninsula to Australia, Australia to Antarctica and at the Drake Passage.

This is a North Polar aspect showing the continents to advantage but with natural boundaries and minimum ocean cuts.

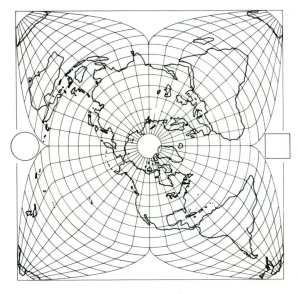

MAP XVA: Polar equal area map of the world cuts all the oceans and Antarctica. The circle and square on either side of the map are each one per-cent of the global area, Gringorten, 1973.

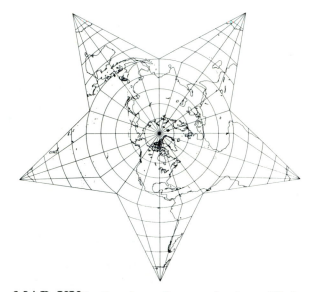

MAP XVB: Berghaus Star projection. All the oceans and the continents of Africa and South America are severely interrupted.

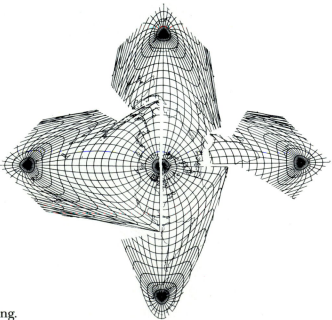

MAP XVC: Diagram of Map XV segment fitting.

MAP XV

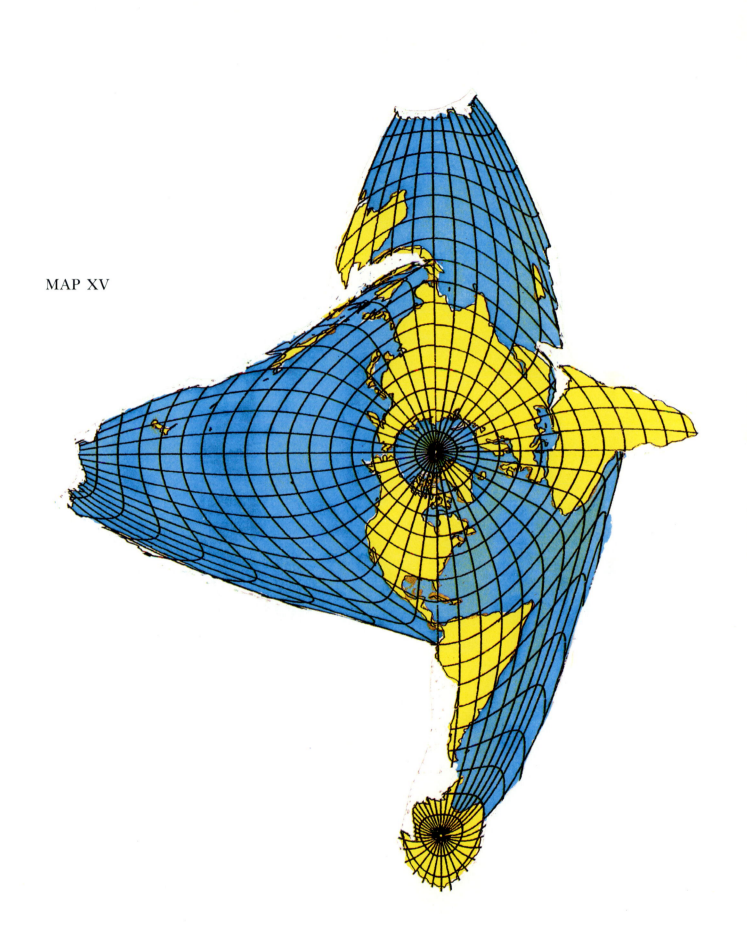

COMPOSITE SHORELINE MAP XVI

Interrupted three-lobed centered transverse sinusoidal equal area with lobes centered at the Equator and central meridians at 60° E. (Indian), 165° W. (Pacific) and 45° W. (Atlantic). Projection poles are on the Equator, 90° E. and 90° W. of central meridians.

This map may be compared with well-known projections (MAPS XVIA and XVIB). It cuts no continents and cuts oceans at minimum junctions only.

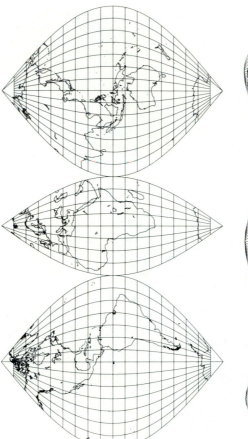
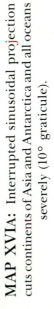

MAP XVIA: Interrupted sinusoidal projection cuts continents of Asia and Antarctica and all oceans severely (10° graticule).

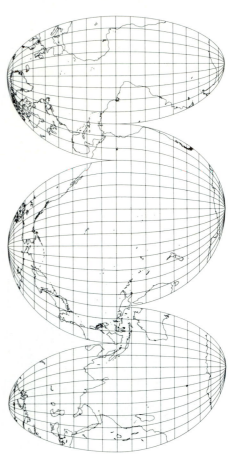

MAP XVIB: Interrupted Mollweide projection cuts all the continents to show oceans to best advantage (10° graticule).

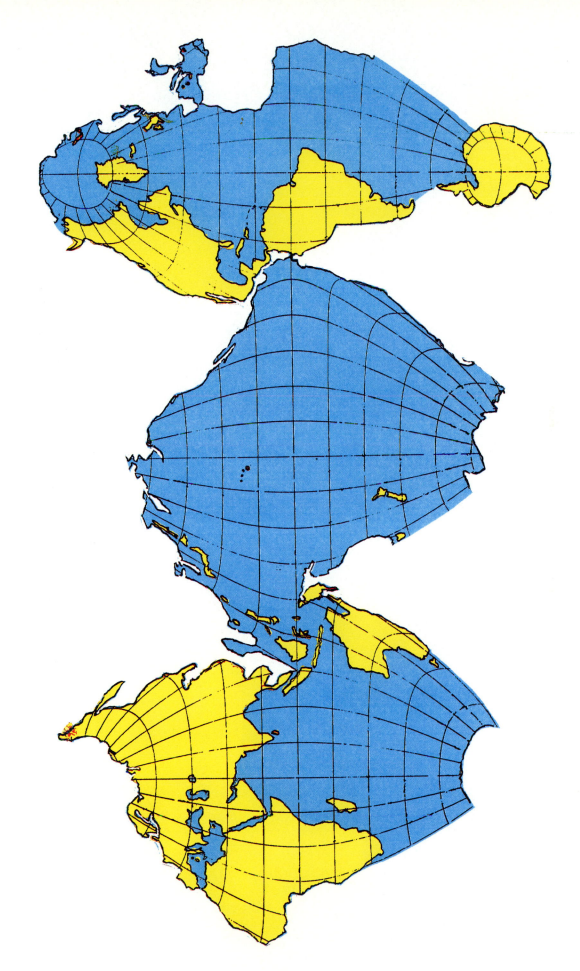

MAP XVI

[47]

COMPOSITE SHORELINE MAP XVII

Composite centered transverse and normal sinusoidal equal area projections with segments centered at the Equator and central meridians as follows: Transverse (1) 15° E., (2) 15° W. and (3) 165° W.; Normal (4) 15° E., (5) 15° W., and (6) 165° E. Projection poles are: Transverse, Equator at 90° E. and 90° W. of central meridians; Normal, 90° N. and 90° S.

This is a variant of common land and water hemisphere maps but with coastline and shortest ocean cut boundaries.

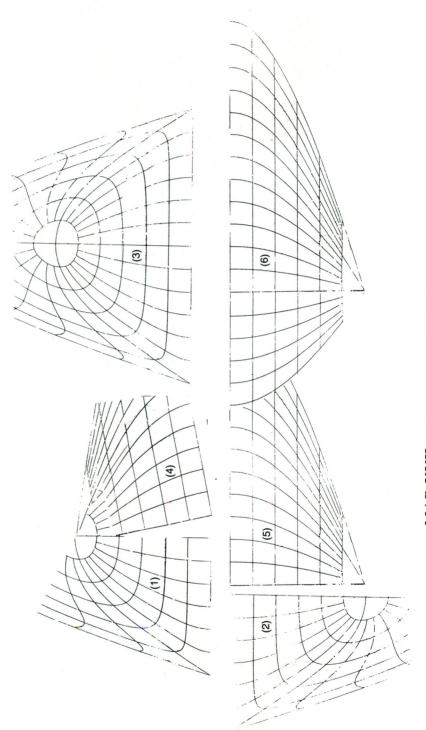

MAP XVIIA: Arrangement of the six segments.

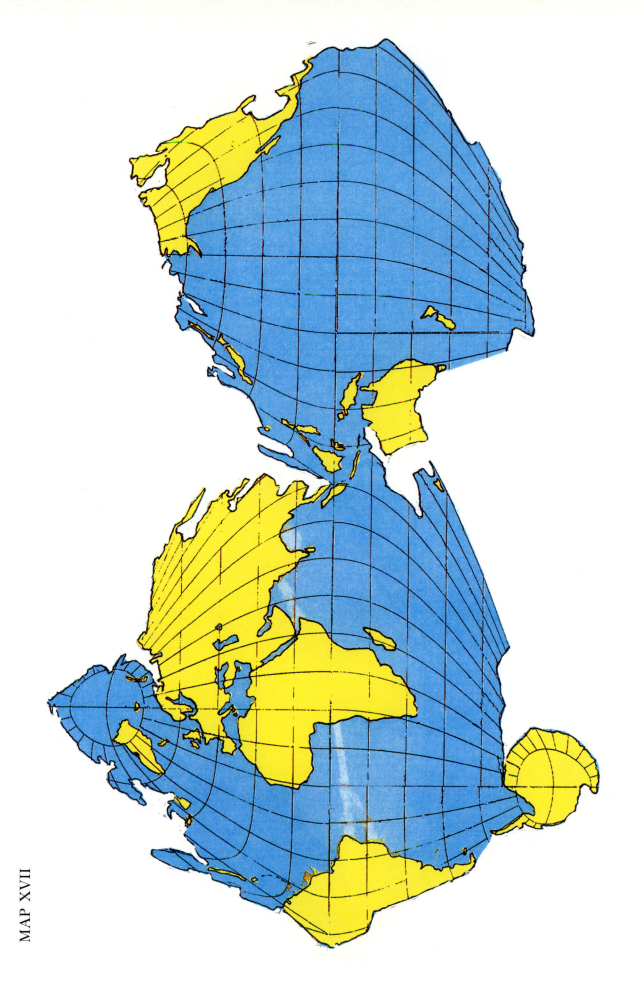

MAP XVII

COMPOSITE SHORELINE MAP XVIII

Composite centered transverse and normal sinusoidal equal area projections with segments centered at the Equator and central meridians as follows: Normal (1) 75° E., (2) 105° E. and (3) 75° W.; Transverse (4) 75° W., (5) 60° W. Projection poles are: Normal, 90° N. and 90° S.; Transverse, 90° E. and 90° W. of the central meridians.

This map shows oceans and continents in their entirety to good advantage. Compare Map XVIIIA which was designed to show land masses but has multiple interruptions in the oceans.

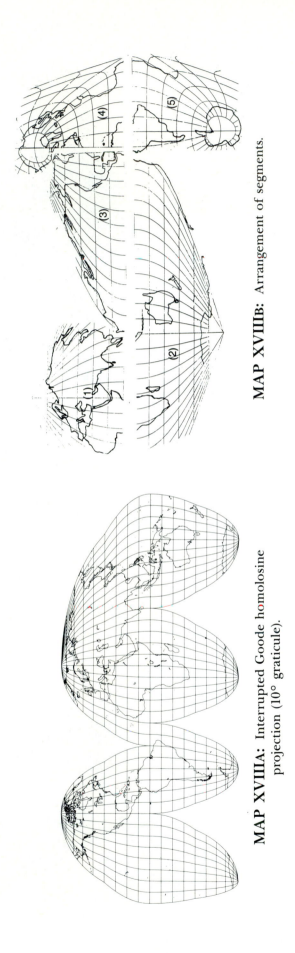

MAP XVIIIA: Interrupted Goode homolosine projection (10° graticule).

MAP XVIIIB: Arrangement of segments.

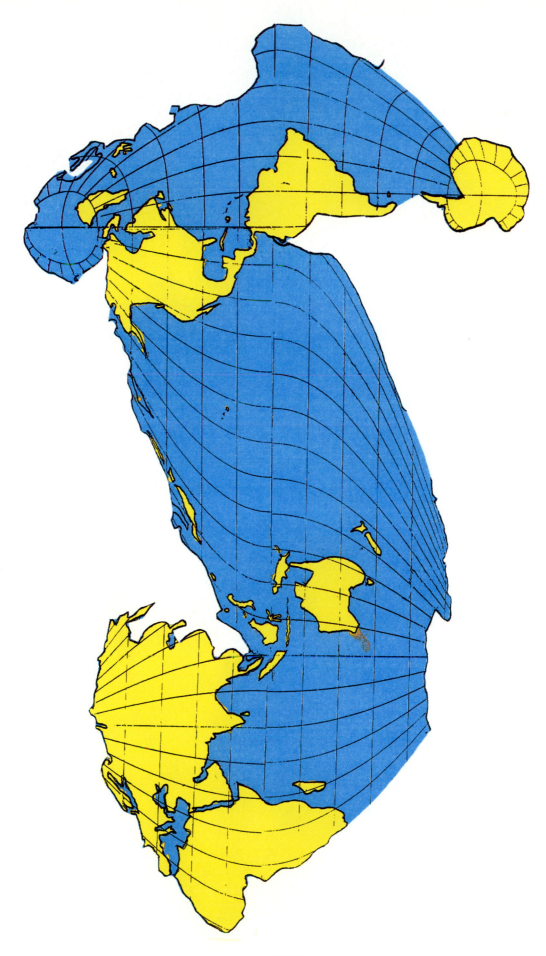

MAP XVIII

COMPOSITE SHORELINE MAP XIX

Composite oblique normal sinusoidal equal area projections. Left half centered at 23° N., 80° E., with projection poles at 67° N., 100° W. and 67° S., 80° E. Right half centered at 17.5° S., 80° E., with projection poles at 72.5° N., 80° E. and 72.5° S., 100° W.

This composite shows both Arctic and Antarctic to good advantage. This map is unique in that it requires double antipodal shoreline coincidences on a single meridian. Such an improbable situation does approximately occur near the 80° E.–100° W. meridian (cf. FIG. 2).

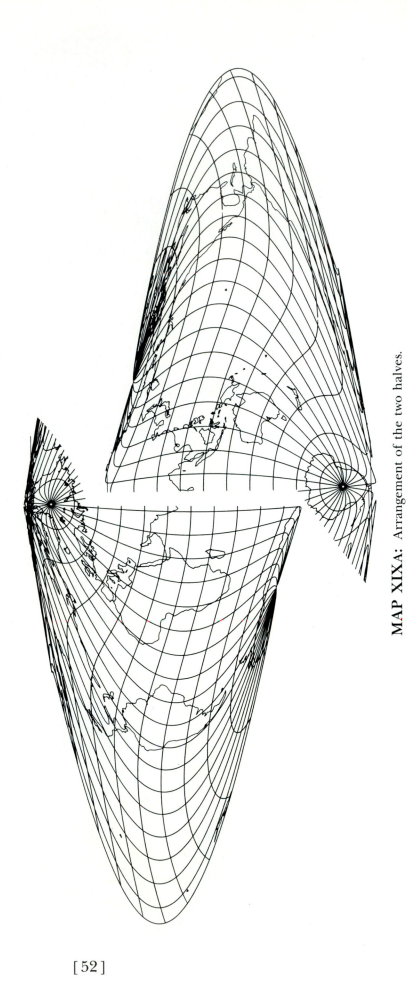

MAP XIXA: Arrangement of the two halves.

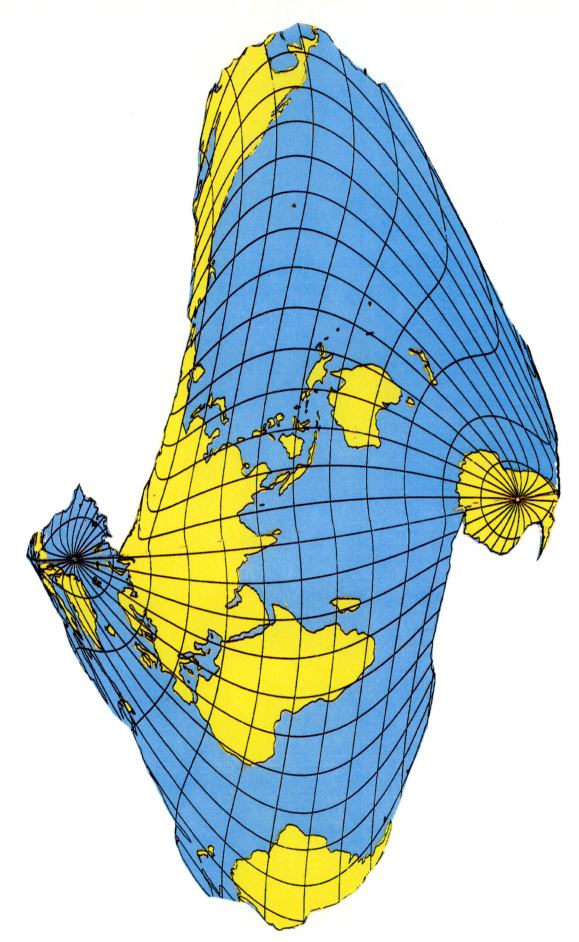

MAP XIX

COMPOSITE SHORELINE MAP XX

Composite of three centered transverse Aitoff compromise projections (neither equal area nor conformal) with centers at: Equator and 55° W. (North America), 65° E. (Asia), 10° E. (Antarctica). Projection poles are at 90° E. and 90° W. of central meridians.

This map could be composed in the same way from sinusoidal (for true equal area) or from other compromise projections (Putnin's P$_5$ and Van der Grinten IV). It shows the versatility of using natural boundaries.

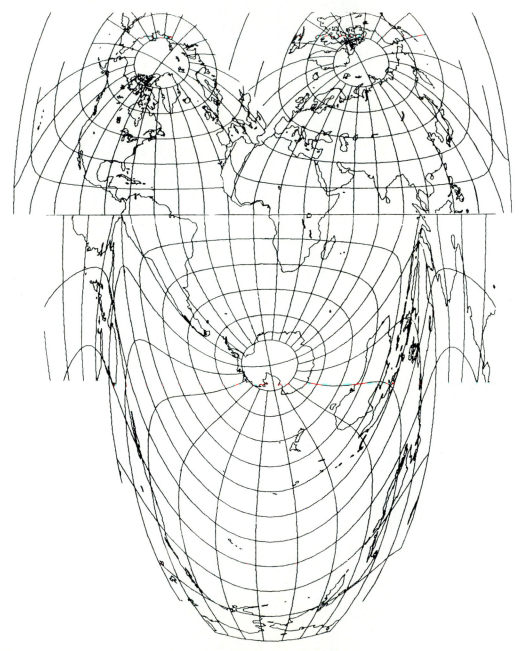

MAP XXA: Composite Aitoff projection with extended graticule, unclipped to show arrangement of the three segments.

[54]

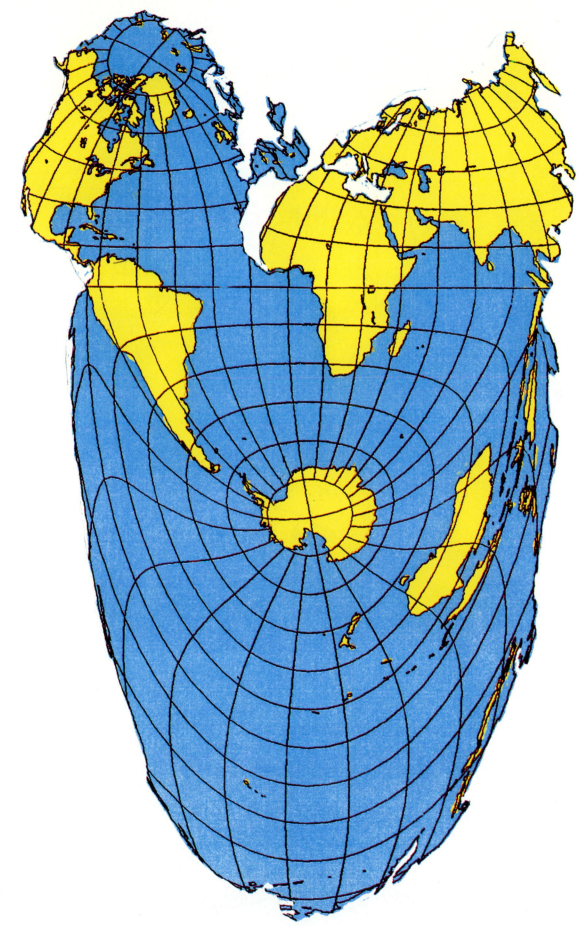

MAP XX

[55]

COMPOSITE SHORELINE MAP XXI

Interrupted azimuthal equidistant projection with centers on the Equator, 10° E. and 170° W. This map shows a spherical segment of more than a hemisphere with the six continents surrounding the Atlantic and Indian Oceans and a spherical segment of less than a hemisphere for the Pacific Ocean alone. Compare to Map XVII.

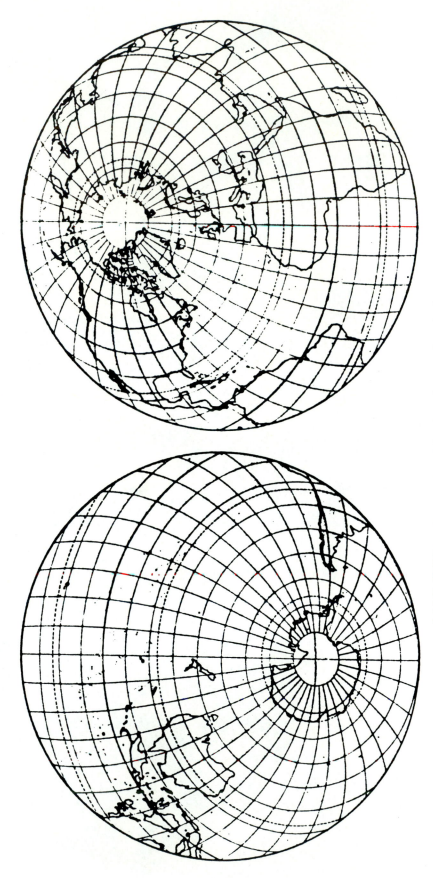

MAP XXIA: Conventional land and water hemispheres.

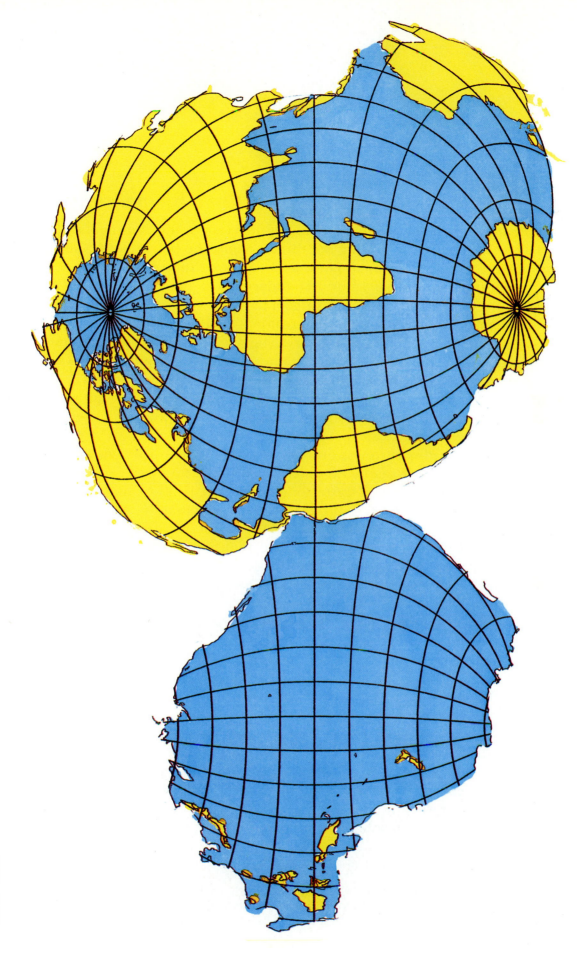

MAP XXI

Tectonic Plate Margins as Natural Boundaries

While the most obvious natural physical boundaries are the continental shorelines and the narrowest connections joining the three oceans, the principle of using natural boundaries instead of the traditional latitude and/or longitude lines as the borders of the maps may be applied to other natural boundaries. The boundaries of the principal tectonic plates are of particular interest in geophysics.

On normal projections such as the Mercator (FIG. 10[12] and MAP XXIIA[13]) and the Mollweide (MAP XXVIIIA, Present) three of the seven large plates are incompletely delineated due to the way the North and South polar regions are shown or omitted. This is a short-coming in the otherwise beautiful and instructive map, "This Dynamic Planet,"[14] compiled by the Smithsonian Institution and the U.S. Geological Survey. The Mercator Projection was used and the error committed on Mercator maps in schoolhouses all over the world, that of calling it a "world map," was perpetuated.

To use the plate margins as the natural boundaries of the world map, it is necessary to find a point on the edge of one plate which is antipodal to a point on another plate boundary. From an antipodal map of the tectonic plates (FIG. 11), two points may be chosen as the poles of an oblique world map projection on an extended graticule as described in the case of the shoreline maps. This antipodal tectonic plate map shows that there are not many choices for the poles. Only a few plate boundary coincidences present themselves, especially for equatorial aspects where the antipodal points must be near the geographic poles and even for transverse aspects where antipodes must be chosen on or near the Equator.

Using these plate boundary coincidences, world maps with plate margins as their edges can be computer drawn.

True world maps (MAPS XXII–XXV) of all the tectonic plates in their entirety may thus be generated, including those plates adjoining the North and South Poles usually transected on normal maps.

Interrupted World Maps of the Tectonic Plates

Just as interrupted maps can be made with natural physical shoreline boundaries, so interrupted maps can be made with tectonic plate boundaries (MAP XXVI). As before, the only advantage of interrupting the world map is to obtain less distortion of the shapes of continents and plates. In all other respects, the uninterrupted maps are preferable.

---

[12] Burke, Kevin and Kidd, W. S. F., "Earth, heat flow in hot-spots," *McGraw-Hill Yearbook of Science and Technology*, McGraw-Hill, New York, pp. 165–9.

[13] *Transactions*, American Geophysical Union, Vol. 71, No. 26, June 26, 1990.

[14] Simkin, T., Tilling, R. I., Taggart, J. N., Jones, W. J., & Spall, H., "This Dynamic Planet, World Map of Volcanoes, Earthquakes and Plate Tectonics," Smithsonian Institution/U.S. Geological Survey, 1989.

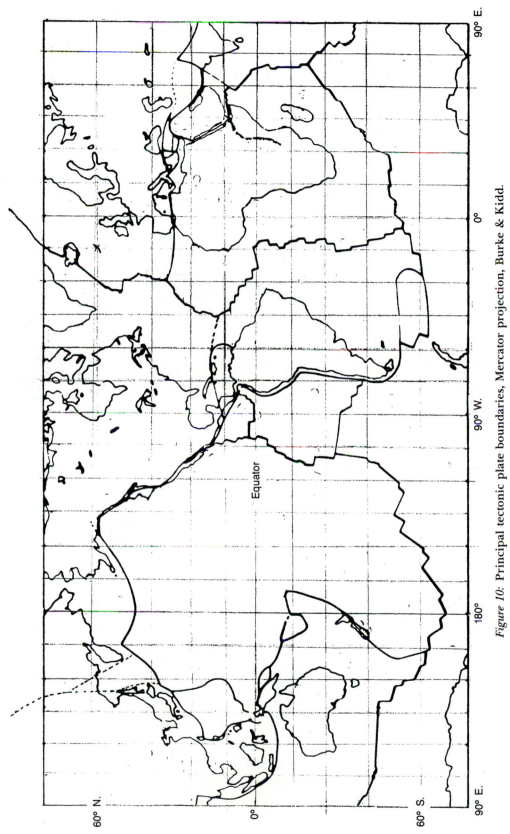

Figure 10: Principal tectonic plate boundaries, Mercator projection, Burke & Kidd.

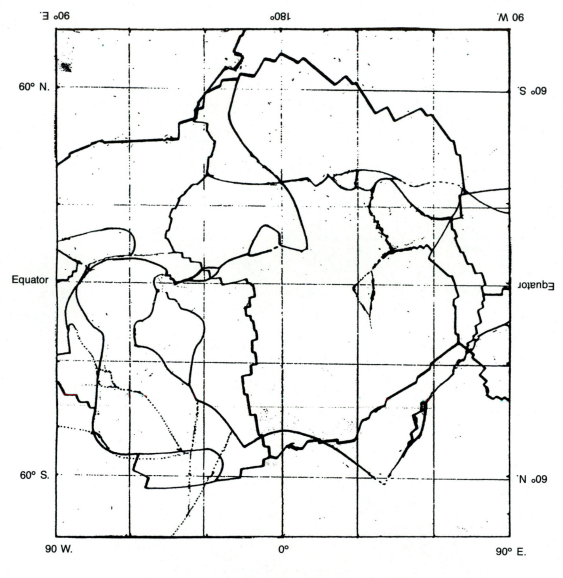

30° graticule

Figure 11: Antipodal tectonic plate map.

Maps with Tectonic Plate Margins
as Natural Boundaries

Maps XXII to XXVI

TECTONIC PLATE MARGIN MAP XXII

Oblique normal Hammer equal area with projection poles at 60° N., 15° W.; 60° S., 165° E.; center at 30° S., 15° W.

This is an equatorial view of the world with plate margins used as the boundaries of the map. All the tectonic plates are shown uncut in their entirety. Compare to Map XXIIA where the Pacific plate is dissected and the North American, Eurasian and Antarctic plates are not only dissected but cannot be shown in their entirety. An additional map is necessary to show the plate boundaries in the vicinity of the North Pole, Map XXIIB.

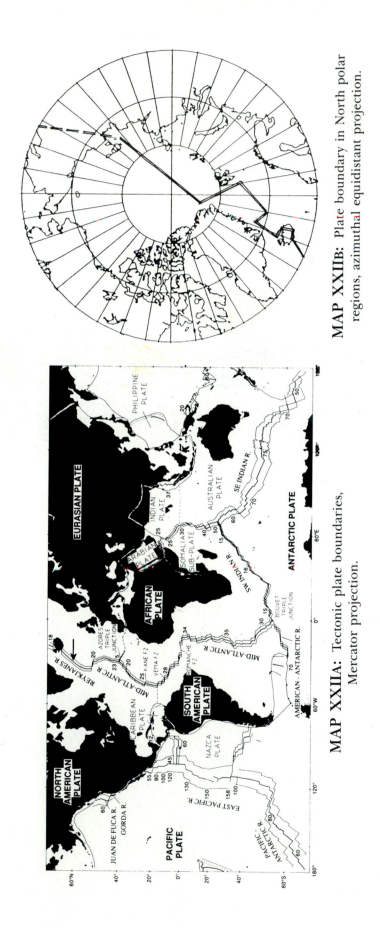

MAP XXIIA: Tectonic plate boundaries, Mercator projection.

MAP XXIIB: Plate boundary in North polar regions, azimuthal equidistant projection.

[62]

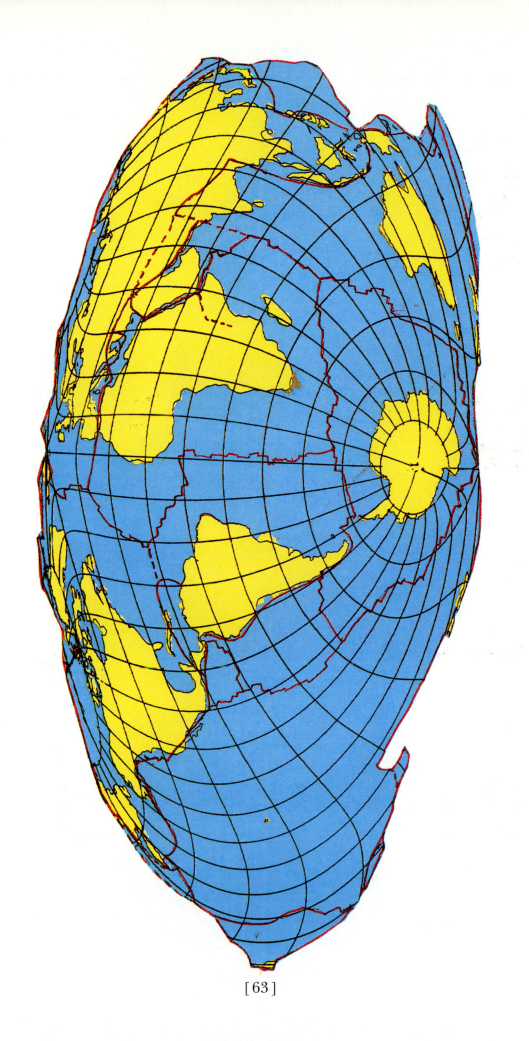

MAP XXII

TECTONIC PLATE MARGIN MAP XXIII

Oblique normal Hammer equal area with projection poles at 60° N., 180°; 60° S., 0°; center at 30° S., 180°.

This map is similar to XXII except that the center of the map has been moved to the 180° meridian to show the "ring of fire" around the Pacific caused by the encroachment of the surrounding tectonic plates. Of course, the "ring of fire" can be viewed from the antipode as being around the leading edges of the plates carrying the continents, Map XXIIIA.

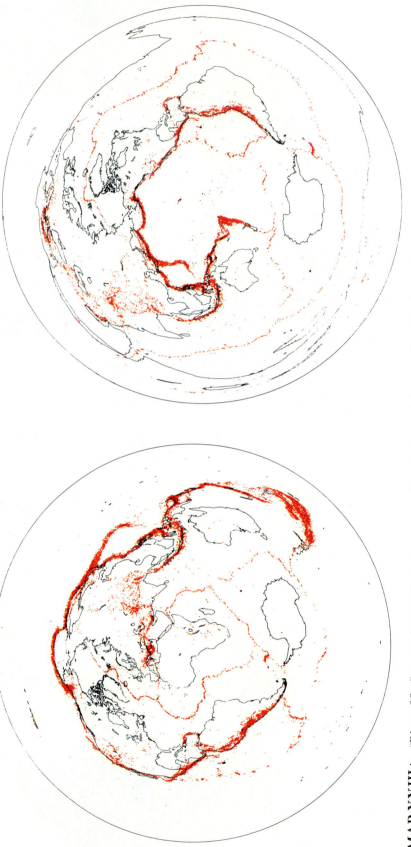

MAP XXIIIA: "Ring of fire" around spreading continents, azimuthal equidistant projection centered on equatorial Africa, Spilhaus, 1975.

MAP XXIIIB: "Ring of fire" around the Pacific, azimuthal equidistant projection centered on equatorial Pacific, Spilhaus, 1975.

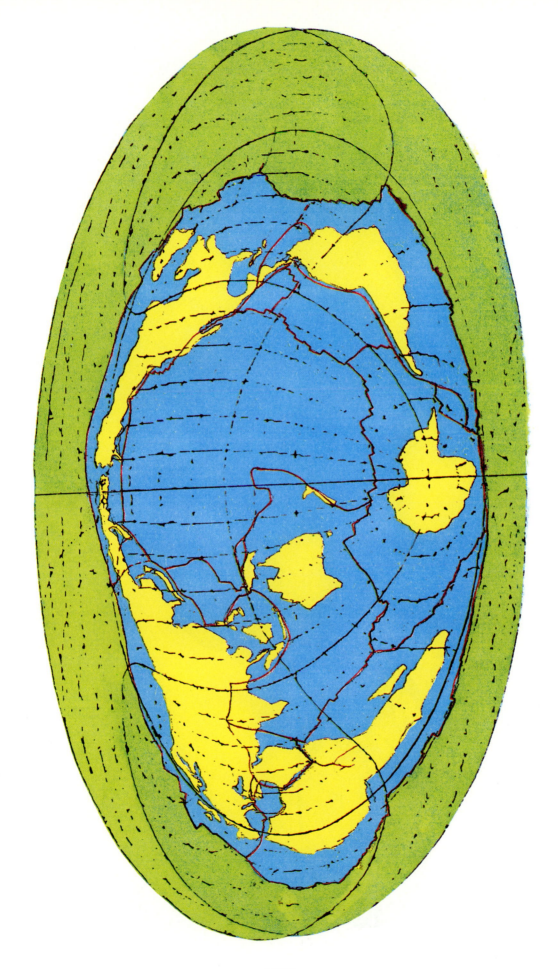

MAP XXIII

TECTONIC PLATE MARGIN MAP XXIV

Oblique normal Hammer equal area with projection poles at 60° N., 0°; 60° S., 180°; center at 30° N., 180°.

This map shows how a slight change of aspect may be used to improve the appearance of the features to be emphasized. Compared to Map XXIII, the shape of the continents, except for Antarctica, has been improved.

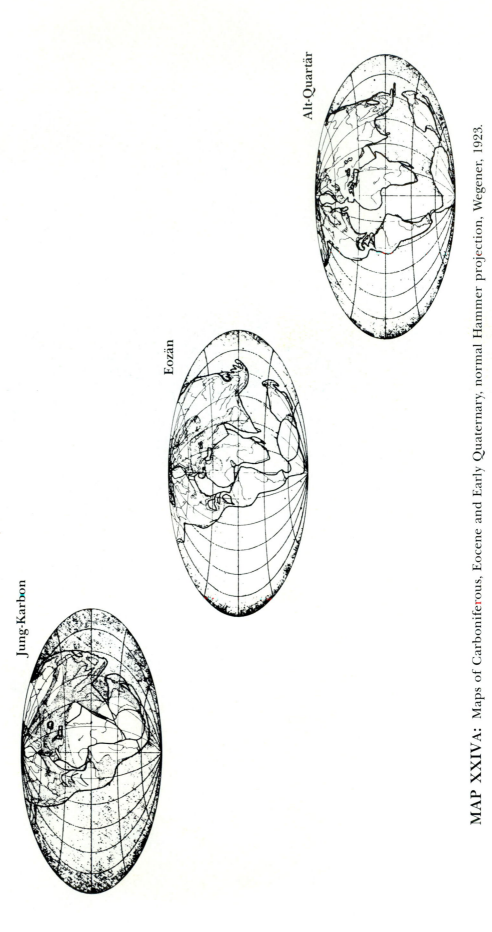

Jung-Karbon

Eozän

Alt-Quartär

MAP XXIVA: Maps of Carboniferous, Eocene and Early Quaternary, normal Hammer projection, Wegener, 1923.

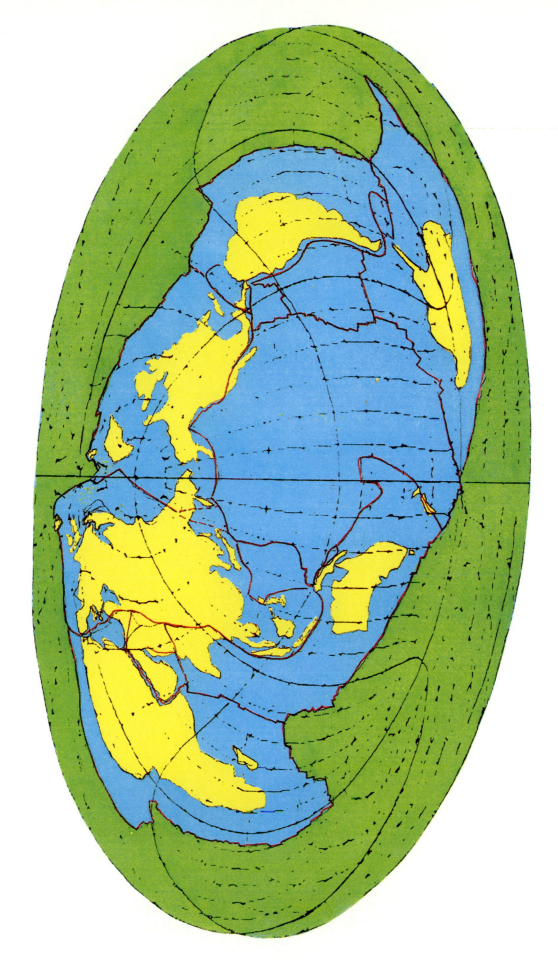

MAP XXIV

[67]

TECTONIC PLATE MARGIN MAP XXV

Centered transverse Hammer equal area with projection poles at Equator and 80° W., 100° E.; center at Equator, 10° E.

This is Map III with the plate boundaries superimposed. This is possible because antipodal plate boundaries and antipodal shorelines both occur at 80° W. and 100° E. on the Equator.

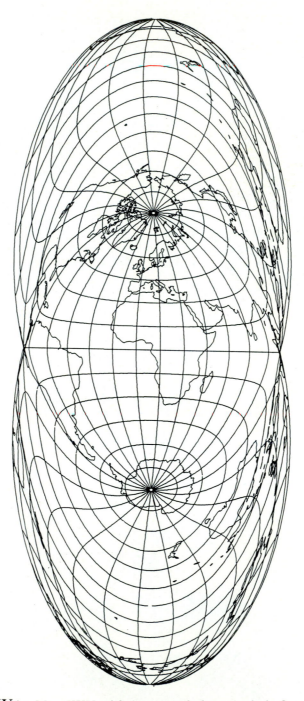

MAP XXVA: Map XXV with its extended graticule before clipping.

MAP XXV

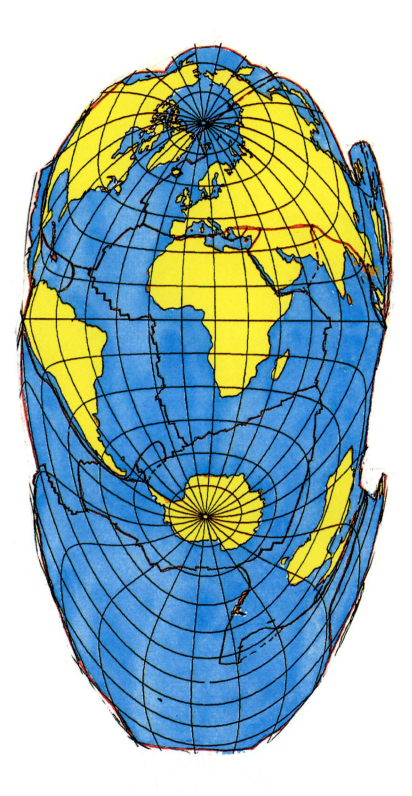

TECTONIC PLATE MARGIN MAP XXVI

Composite of two normal transverse sinusoidal equal area projections with lobes centered at 90° S. (South Pole) and central meridians 90° W.–90° E. and 0°–180°. Projection poles are on the Equator, 90° E. and 90° W. of central meridians.

This map, similar to Map XV but centered on the South Pole, suggested the construction of a jigsaw map of the tectonic plates. The jigsaw is arranged so that the continents can be moved from their present positions to their positions at the time of the supercontinent of Pangea. The projection on the tetrahedron permits the pieces of the puzzle to tessellate and a complete map of the world may be made with about two hundred different aspects.

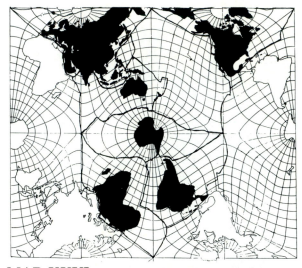

MAP XXVIA: Lee conformal tetrahedric projection with severe liberties to allow the tetrahedral apices to coincide with plate boundaries.

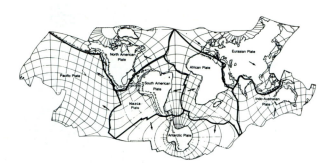

MAP XXVIB: "Puzzle of the Plates," tessellating jigsaw map of the world with tectonic plate margins as natural boundaries. Lee conformal tetrahedric projection with severe liberties to cause the tetrahedral apices to coincide with plate boundaries; Spilhaus, U.S. Patent 4,627,622; American Geophysical Union, 1984.

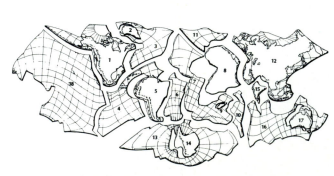

MAP XXVIC: "Puzzle of the Plates," individual pieces.

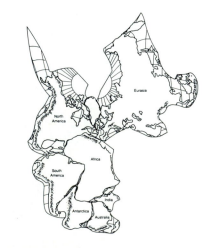

MAP XXVID: "Puzzle of the Plates," individual pieces arranged to show Pangea (178 million years ago).

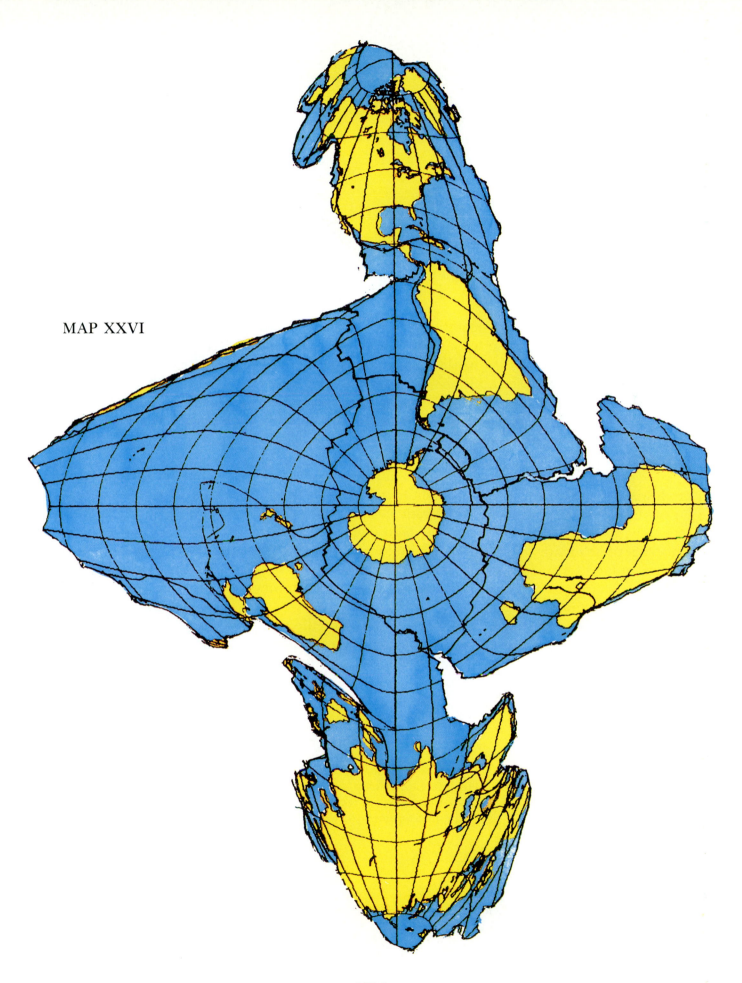

MAP XXVI

Movement of Land Masses through Geologic Time

To show the movement, accretion and separation of masses of land through geologic time is a challenge in cartography. Although tectonophysicists talk about absolute motion of the surface features of the world throughout time, the fixed reference of this absolute motion is not yet clear. Certainly, the spin axis of the Earth from north to south geographic pole is one that can be accepted. Therefore, a projection that can encompass the maximum motion along the meridians relative to the geographic poles is desirable. This should be a transverse projection because the transverse aspect provides 360° of movement along any meridian.

A normal projection has only 180° latitude for motion along the meridian. In the following maps showing the movement of land masses through geologic time, a centered transverse projection with extended graticule has been used as the basic projection (FIG. 12).

The data for the positions of the land masses in geologic time are taken from Scotese.[15] Scotese's maps on a normal Mollweide projection show the positions of the major pieces of land from the Early Cambrian, 555 million years ago, to the Present. However, these maps cut the land masses in past times so much that they are almost unrecognizable (MAPS XXVIIA and XXVIIIA).

The transverse projection with extended graticule preserves the unity of the land masses and gives a far more understandable picture of plate movement, (MAPS XXVII and XXVIII). It is instructive to superimpose maps of different geologic epochs to obtain a "moving picture" of the positions of the drifting land masses through the ages (MAP XXIX).

Of all of this did Plato speak,
   In reference to map and chart,
A legacy from classic Greek,
   "The measurement of Earth is Art."[16]

---

[15] Scotese, Christopher R., et al., "Atlas of Phanerozoic Plate Tectonic Reconstructions," American Geophysical Union, (in press).

[16] Spilhaus, Athelstan, 1990.

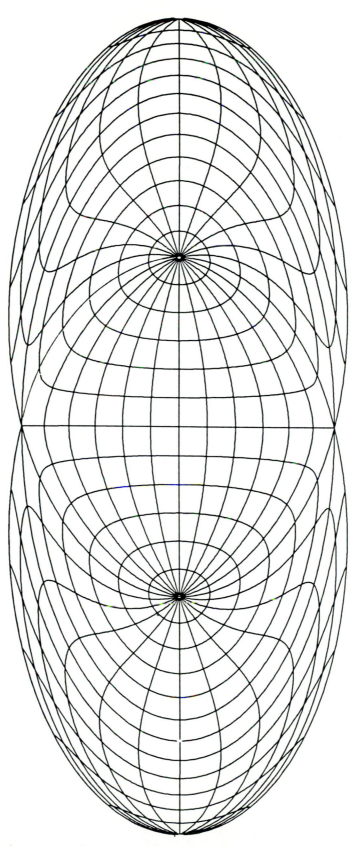

Figure 12: Centered transverse Hammer equal area graticule extended to encompass "1½" worlds.

Movement of Land Masses
through Geologic Time

Maps XXVII to XXIX

TECTONIC PLATE MARGIN MAP XXVII

Centered transverse Hammer equal area with projection poles at Equator and 100° E., 80° W.; center at Equator, 10° E.

These maps show the positions of land masses for three eras: Early Cambrian (555 million years ago), Ordovician (478 million years ago) and Westphalian (306 million years ago). The corresponding maps of Scotese, from which the data were taken, are shown (MAP XXVIIA).

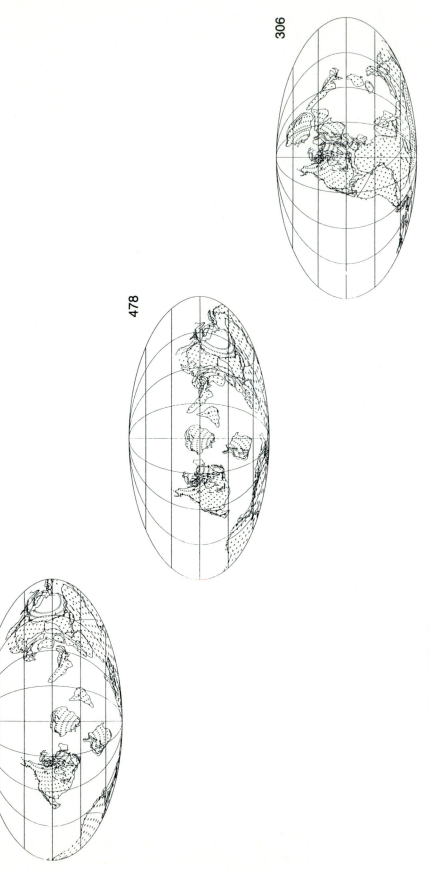

MAP XXVIIA: Phanerozoic plate tectonic reconstructions by Scotese; normal Mollweide.

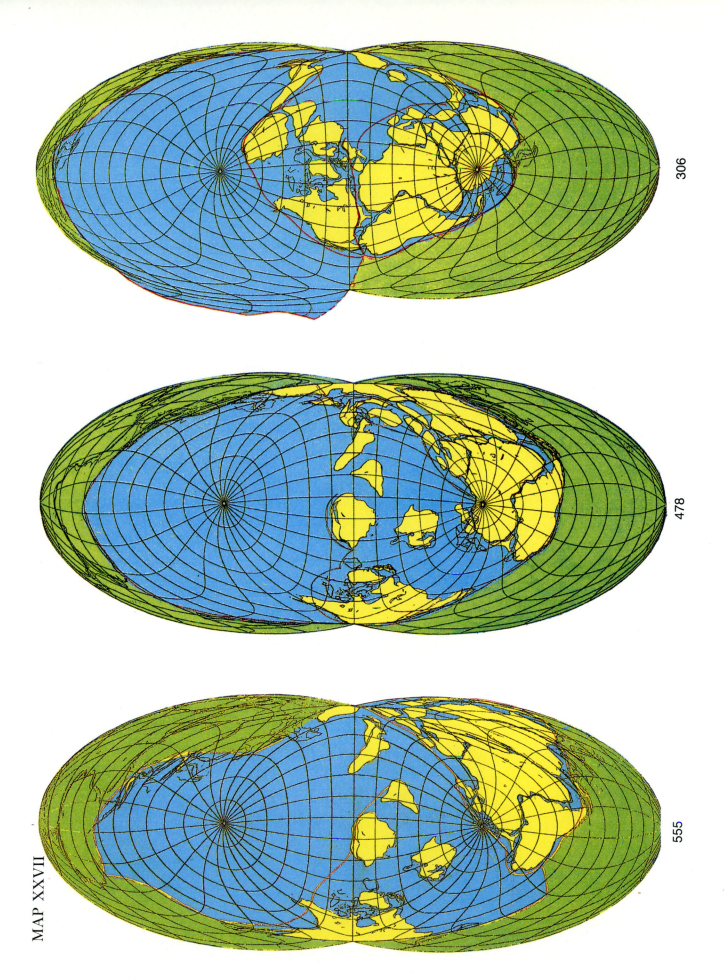

MAP XXVII

306

478

555

TECTONIC PLATE MARGIN MAP XXVIII

Centered transverse Hammer equal area with projection poles at Equator and 100° E, 80° W; center at Equator, 10° E.

These maps continue the sequence and show subsequent positions of land masses for three eras: Oxfordian (160 million years ago), Danian (65 million years ago) and the Present. The corresponding maps of Scotese, from which the data were taken, are shown (MAP XXVIIIA).

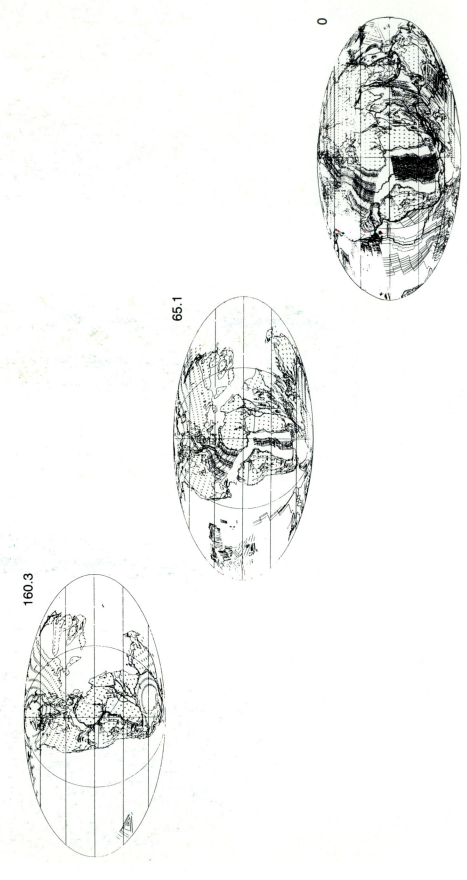

160.3

65.1

0

MAP XXVIIIA: Phanerozoic plate tectonic reconstructions by Scotese; normal Mollweide.

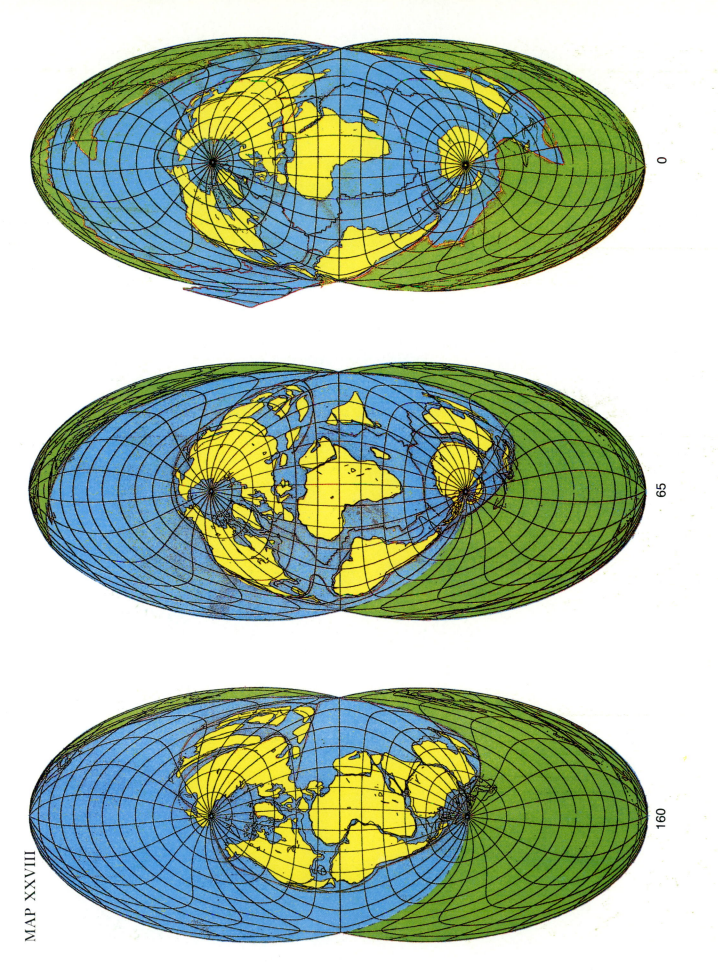

MAP XXVIII

0

65

160

[79]

TECTONIC PLATE MARGIN MAP XXIX

Centered transverse Hammer equal area with projection poles at Equator and 100° E., 80° W.; center at Equator, 10° E.

This map shows the positions of land masses for three eras from the oldest to the present: Early Cambrian (555 million years ago), Late Carboniferous (306 million years ago) and the Present. The three are superimposed on the expanded graticule, a storyboard for the movement of landmasses through time.

Earth's Changing Face is always young
And every line has meaning.
Her portrait we have just begun;
The End—A new beginning.

MAP XXIX

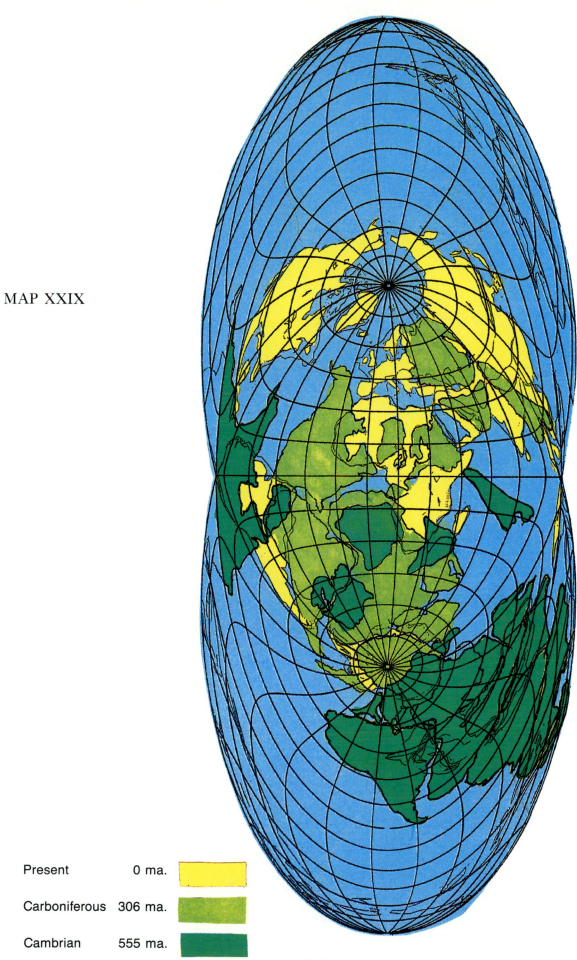

Present	0 ma.	
Carboniferous	306 ma.	
Cambrian	555 ma.	

Figure and Map Credits

TEXT FIGURES:

3.	"Smithsonian," Nov., 1979, p. 120.
7.	Base projection Snyder & Voxland, *Album*, p. 161.
10.	Plate boundaries and geography, Burke & Kidd.

MAPS:

IA.	"Geographical Review."
IIIA.	Snyder & Voxland, *Album*, p. 56.
IVA.	Snyder & Voxland, *Album*, p. 161.
VIA.	Snyder & Voxland, *Album*, p. 163.
VIIA.	U.S. State Department.
VIIB.	McBryde.
VIIIA.	"Geographical Review."
IXA.	Snyder & Voxland, *Album*, p. 187.
XA.	Snyder & Voxland, *Album*, p. 181.
XIIA.	*Proceedings of the American Philosophical Society* Vol. 127, No. 1, 1983, pp. 52, 58.
XIIIA.	"Smithsonian," Nov., 1979, p. 120.
XIVA.	"Smithsonian," Nov., 1979, p. 122.
XVA.	"Air Force Surveys in Geophysics," No. 269, 4 June 1973.
XVB.	Snyder & Voxland, *Album*, p. 157.
XVIA.	Snyder & Voxland, *Album*, p. 43.
XVIB.	Snyder & Voxland, *Album*, p. 57.
XVIIIA.	Snyder & Voxland, *Album*, p. 67.
XXIIA.	"EOS," *Transactions*, American Geophysical Union, Vol. 71, No. 26, June 26, 1990, cover illustration.
XXIIIA.	"EOS," *Transactions*, American Geophysical Union, Vol. 56, No. 2, Feb., 1975, cover illustration.
XXIIIB.	"EOS," *Transactions*, American Geophysical Union, Vol. 56, No. 2, Feb., 1975, cover illustration.
XXIVA.	Marvin, Ursula B., *Continental Drift, The Evolution of a Concept*, Smithsonian Institution Press, Washington, D.C., 1973, p. 75.
XXVIA.	*Proceedings of the American Philosophical Society*, Vol. 128, No. 3, 1984, p. 262.
XXVIB.	"Puzzle of the Plates," American Geophysical Union, 1985.
XXVIC.	"Puzzle of the Plates," American Geophysical Union, 1985.
XXVID.	"Puzzle of the Plates," American Geophysical Union, 1985.
XXVIIA.	Scotese, Christopher, *Phanerozoic Plate Tectonic Reconstructions*, University of Texas, 1987.
XXVIIIA.	Scotese, Christopher, *Phanerozoic Plate Tectonic Reconstructions*, University of Texas, 1987.

Bibliography

Burke, Kevin & Dewey, J. F., "Plume Generated Triple Junctions: Key Indicators in Applying Plate Tectonics to Old Rocks," *The Journal of Geology*, Vol. 81, No. 4, University of Chicago, July, 1973.

Burke, Kevin and Kidd, W. S. F., "Earth, heat flow in hot-spots," *McGraw-Hill Yearbook of Science and Technology*, McGraw-Hill, New York, pp. 165–9.

Deetz, Charles H., *Cartography, A Review and Guide for the Construction and Use of Maps and Charts*, U.S. Dept. of Commerce Special Publication No. 205, U.S. Government Printing Office, Washington, D.C., 1943.

Deetz, Charles H. & Adams, Oscar S., *Elements of Map Projections, with Applications to Map and Chart Construction*, Fifth Edition, U.S. Dept. of Commerce Special Publication No. 68, U.S. Government Printing Office, Washington, D.C., 1945.

Gringorten, Irving I., "A Polar Equal-Area Map of the World," *Air Force Surveys in Geophysics*, No. 269, 4 June 1973.

Hallam, A., "Alfred Wegener and the Hypothesis of Continental Drift," *Scientific American*, New York.

Liu, HanShou, "On the Breakup of Tectonic Plates by Polar Wandering," Goddard Space Flight Center, Greenbelt, Maryland, August, 1973.

Marvin, Ursula B., *Continental Drift, The Evolution of a Concept*, Smithsonian Institution Press, Washington, D.C., 1973, p. 75.

Melluish, R. K., *An Introduction to the Mathematics of Map Projections*, Cambridge University Press, Cambridge, 1931.

Richardus, Peter & Adler, Ron K., *Map Projections*, North Holland Publishing Co., Amsterdam, 1972.

Schmid, Erwin, "World Maps on the August Epicycloidal Conformal Projection," NOAA Technical Report NOS 63, U.S. Dept. of Commerce, Rockville, MD, May 1974.

Scotese, Christopher, *Phanerozoic Plate Tectonic Reconstructions*, University of Texas, 1987.

———, et al., *Atlas of Phanerozoic Plate Tectonic Reconstructions*, American Geophysical Union, in press.

——— & Denham, Charles R., "User's Manual for Terra Mobilis: Plate Tectonics for the Macintosh," C. R. Scotese and C. R. Denham, 1988.

Simkin, T., Tilling, R. I., Taggart, J. N., Jones, W. J., & Spall, H., "This Dynamic Planet, World Map of Volcanoes, Earthquakes and Plate Tectonics," Smithsonian Institution/U.S. Geological Survey, 1989.

Smith, A. G., & Briden, J. C., *Mesozoic and Cenozoic Paleocontinental Maps*, Cambridge University Press, Cambridge, 1977.

Snyder, John P., *Map Projections—A Working Manual*, U.S. Geological Survey, Professional Paper No. 1395, U.S. Government Printing Office, Washington, D.C., 1987.

Snyder, John P., and Voxland, Philip M., *An Album of Map Projections*, U.S. Geological Survey, Professional Paper 1453, U.S. Government Printing Office, Washington, D.C., 1989.

Spilhaus, Athelstan, "Maps of the whole world ocean," *Geographical Review*, 32:431–35, July, 1942.

———. "Geo-Art: Plate Tectonics and Platonic Solids," EOS, *Transactions*, American Geophysical Union, Vol. 56, No. 2, Feb., 1975, pp. 52–57.

————. "New look in maps brings out patterns of plate tectonics," *Smithsonian*, August, 1976, pp. 54–63.

————. "To see the oceans, slice up the land," *Smithsonian*, November, 1979, pp. 157–163.

————. "A New Way of Looking at the World," *Calypso Log*, September, 1981, p. 12.

————. "Be the First to Sail Straight Around the World—Almost!" *Virginia Country*, Winter, 1981, pp. 48–49.

————. "World Ocean Maps: The Proper Places to Interrupt," *Proceedings of the American Philosophical Society*, Vol. 127, No. 1, 1983, pp. 50–60.

————. "An equal area map of the world with edges formed by major tectonic plate boundaries," EOS, *Transactions*, American Geophysical Union, Vol. 64, No. 14, Apr. 5, 1983.

————. "Plate Tectonics in Geoforma and Jigsaws," *Proceedings of the American Philosophical Society*, Vol. 128, No. 3, 1984, pp. 257–269.

————. "The Puzzle of the Plates," American Geophysical Union, 1985.

————. "The Water Planet Map," *Dolphin Log*, March, 1989, pp. 6–7.

————, & Snyder, John, P., "World Maps with Natural Boundaries," *Cartography and Geographic Information Systems*, in press.

Wray, Thomas, "The Seven Aspects of a General Map Projection," Monograph No. 11/1974, *Cartographica*, Supplement No. 2 to "Canadian Cartographer," Vol. 11, University of Toronto Press, 1974.

Glossary

Antipodes: Points diametrically opposite each other on a sphere.

Aspect: The apparent position with respect to the observer. In cartography, the world may be turned on its axis or the axis tilted to provide different "aspects." Aspect is the choice of what the artist wants the viewer to see. It is what puts "art" in *cart*ography.

Azimuth: The horizontal direction expressed as the angular distance between the direction of a fixed point and the direction of the object.

Azimuthal equidistant projection: A map projection so centered at any given point that a straight line radiating from the center to any other point represents the shortest distance and can be measured accurately.

Centered transverse aspect: Aspect with the same center as the normal aspect, at the intersection of the Equator and the straight central meridian, and projection poles on the Equator 90° east and west.

Centered oblique aspect: Aspect centered at 0° latitude on the central meridian at the Equator with projection poles on the 90th meridian of the normal aspect.

Central meridian: The line of longitude which passes through the center of the projection.

Composite projections: Formed by connecting two or more projections along common lines. Composites can include combinations of different aspects of the same projection.

Compromise projections: Do not strictly preserve regular features, such as equal area, conformal, or equidistant, but average two features in an attempt to present the best of both.

Conformal projections: Have the same scale along both the meridian and the parallel at any point and have meridians and parallels at right angles so that the shapes of small areas around that point are true to the shape of the corresponding areas on the Earth.

Continental shoreline coincidences: Points of antipodal correspondence which fall on the shorelines of continents.

Distortion: A lack of proportionality between corresponding dimensions which may result in variation of angle, scale or area.

Epicycloidal projection: A conformal projection where the boundary of the world map is a curve traced by a point on a circle that rolls on the outside of a fixed circle.

Equal area projection: A projection which maintains a constant ratio of size between quadrilaterals formed by the meridians and parallels and the quadrilaterals of the globe thereby preserving true areal extent of forms represented; also called equivalent or authalic. Shapes are distorted.

Equatorial view: A map where the Equator is more or less horizontal.

Geographic poles: The north and south poles of the earth's spin axis.

Graticule: The network of latitude and longitude lines on which a map is drawn.

[87]

Great circle: A circle formed on the surface of a sphere by the intersection of a plane that passes through the center of the sphere, specifically, such a circle on the surface of the earth of which an arc constitutes the shortest distance between any two points. The Equator and all meridians are great circles.

Interrupted projection: Does not have continuous outlines but is split (as along meridians or other boundaries) so as to give better shape and scale for continents or oceans.

Isobath: A line on a map connecting all points having the same depth below the surface.

Isopleth: A line on a map along which there is a constant value showing the occurrence or frequency of a phenomenon as a function of two variables.

Isotherm: A line on a map connecting points having the same temperature at a given time or the same mean temperature for a given period.

Loxodrome: A line on the surface of the earth that makes equal angles with all meridians. It is a spherical spiral coiling around the poles but never reaching them. In navigation, it is called a rhumb line, the path of a ship sailing in the direction of the same compass point.

Lune: The part of a spherical surface bounded by two great circles intersecting at an angle.

Mercator projection: The only map were rhumb lines (loxodromes) between any two points are straight lines and at the correct azimuth. It also has the property of conformality.

Meridian: A great circle passing through the poles, a line of longitude.

Normal aspect: Aspect with the simplest graticule. In this atlas, the normal aspect is centered at the intersection of the Equator and the straight central meridian with North and South Poles at the top and bottom.

Oblique normal aspect: Centered on the straight central meridian of the normal projection at any latitude other than 90° or 0° with projection poles on that meridian 90° of latitude from the center.

Oblique transverse aspect: Centered on the straight Equator of the normal projection at any longitude other than 90° or 0° with projection poles on the 90th meridian.

Oblique centered aspect: See centered oblique aspect.

Oblique aspect: Center and projection poles neither on the Equator nor on either the prime central meridian or on the 90th meridian.

Orthogonal: Lying or intersecting at right angles.

Parallel: A line of latitude parallel to the Equator, which is also a parallel.

Parent projection: The origin or source of a derivative aspect.

Plate boundary coincidences: Points of antipodal correspondence which fall on tectonic plate boundaries.

Polar view: A map where one of the geographic poles is more or less in the center.

Prime meridian: 0° longitude, the meridian passing through the original site of the Royal Observatory at Greenwich, England.

Projection: A systematic presentation of intersecting coordinate lines on a flat surface (cf. graticule) on which features from the curved surface of the earth may be mapped.

Projection poles: Any two antipodal points. The North and South geographic poles are projection poles only on normal aspects.

Rhumb line: See loxodrome.

"Ring of Fire:" The common name for the belt of marked tectonic activity, specifically volcanos and earthquakes, at the edges of the continental plates which encircle the Pacific Ocean.

Sinusoidal projection: In normal aspect, an equal area projection showing the entire surface of the earth with all parallels as straight lines evenly spaced, the central meridian as ½ the length of the Equator and the other meridians as curved lines.

Spherical segment: That portion of a sphere between two parallel planes.

Spin axis: The axis of rotation of the earth.

Stereographic projection: Shows latitude and longitude lines projected onto a tangent plane by radials from a point antipodal to the point of tangency. Less than the entire sphere can be shown.

Tectonic plates: Sections of the crust of the earth which are moved on the surface by convection cells below.

Tectonophysics: A branch of geophysics that deals with the forces responsible for movements in and deformation of the earth's crust.

Transverse aspect: One on which the axis of the Earth is rotated 90°.

Transverse normal aspect: Centered at a geographic pole with projection poles on the Equator 90° east and west.

Index